A.C. Keough.
Dec. 2001.

Budapest

A CITY GUIDE

by

Annabel Barber &
Emma Roper-Evans

2nd Edition

SOMERSET LIMITED

© 2001 Somerset Kft.
Vörösmarty tér 1, Pf. 71
1051 Budapest, Hungary
Felelős kiadó: Ruszin Zsolt, a Somerset Kft. igazgatója
office@visiblecities.net
www.visiblecities.net
Visible Cities is a registered trademark.

Layout & Design: *Regina Rácz*
Photographs:
Hadley Kincade, Attila Kleb, Tibor Mester,
Jenő Detvay, Miklós Gellért, Ferenc Kiss,
Jeannette Goehring, Thomas Howells,
Annabel Barber, Andrea Felvégi
Diagrams: *Michael Mansell RIBA*
Maps: *Dimap Bt.*
Repro Studio: *Overprint Kft.*
Printed by: *Novoprint Rt. Attila Miseje, Director.*

Acknowledgements:
With special thanks to the Budapest History Museum,
Hungarian National Museum, Nóra Magyar, István Barkóczi,
Éva Galambos, Bálint Kamarás, Gabriella Klemm,
Toby Mansel-Pleydell, Andrew Spira

Other titles in the Visible Cities series:
Visible Cities Dubrovnik
Further titles are in preparation.

Cover illustration: *Detail from a stained glass window in Andrássy út,*
probably the work of Miksa Róth (1865-1944).
Previous page: *Late 19th-century caryatid (Andrássy út).*

Annabel Barber has lived in Budapest since 1992. A former editor at Budapest
Magazines and food and wine columnist on *The Budapest Business Journal*, she
now works as a freelance writer and translator. Emma Roper-Evans has lived in
Hungary for ten years. In 1996 she received the Milan Füst Prize from the
Hungarian Academy of Sciences for her literary translations.

ISBN 963 00 5929 0

5

CONTENTS

INTRODUCTION

"Buda-Pesth seems a wonderful place... The impression I had was that we were leaving the West and entering the East; the most Western of splendid bridges over the Danube, which is here of noble width and depth, took us among the traditions of Turkish rule..."

With those words, Bram Stoker opens one of the most famous stories of all time: *Dracula*. Jonathan Harker chugs unwittingly towards the Carpathians, taking notes on the sights along the way. And he was right about one thing: Budapest *is* a wonderful place, bisected by the mighty Danube into Buda to the west, leafy and hilly, and Pest to the east, built on a completely flat plain, "straight as a die, like the honour, openness and honesty which so characterises the Hungarian people", as one self-congratulatory writer put it. The same writer continues: "Budapest is supremely graced by nature, and even Naples, which one is enjoined to 'see and die', though it might outdo us in azure sea and sky, has nothing like our city's panorama". He has a point. Budapest's Danube panorama ranks as one of the loveliest cityscapes in Europe.

HOW TO USE THIS GUIDE

General practical information about Budapest is given below. After that the book is divided into four sections. Part I contains historical background to the city and its history. Part II contains detailed information on where to go and what to see, divided into topic categories of particular relevance to Budapest, for example thermal baths and coffee houses, as well as key places of historical and cultural interest. Part III consists of eight guided centre-of-town walks, lasting an average of 45 minutes to an hour each. Part IV contains practical information about the city, as well as an overview of food and wine, with selective lists of restaurants and hotels. A detailed map of the centre of town can be found at the back of the book, with grid references to major streets and sights.

The main ticket hall of Nyugati Railway Station, built by the architects who designed the Eiffel Tower.

CITY LAYOUT

Eight great bridges span the Danube, the three most central being Margaret Bridge (Margit híd), the Chain Bridge (Lánchíd, *see p. 30*), Elisabeth Bridge (Erzsébet híd) and Szabadság (Freedom) híd. As long as you orientate to the river, which flows north-south, you can never really get lost in Budapest. Castle Hill, which rises on the Buda bank to the west, was from mediaeval times right up until the First World War the site of the Hungarian Royal Palace. Facing Castle Hill, with typical Pest grandiloquence, is the enormous Hungarian Parliament, built in neo-Gothic style at the turn of the last century. Budapest is divided into numbered districts, each designated by a Roman numeral, though some of them are also known by evocative names such as Angyalföld (Angel Land), Víziváros (Water Town), or eponymous titles like Lipótváros (Leopold Town) and Józsefváros (Joseph Town). The latter two were named in honour of Habsburg rulers, while the Víziváros was once an area of docks, subject to flooding before the Danube was banked up. Angyalföld was named after a statue of a heavenly creature which once stood there - although as one of the roughest areas of the city, perhaps "Fallen Angel Land" would be a more appropriate name.

The Chain Bridge in the 1890s.

PUBLIC HOLIDAYS

Long gone are the days when the underground band Trabant had a hit song listing the endless Leninist holidays that were celebrated. Today's national holidays are strictly Hungarian in origin, the most honoured being March 15th, August 20th, and October 23rd. The former celebrates the doomed revolution of 1848-9, when

The funicular railway (sikló) that goes from the head of the Chain Bridge up to Castle Hill.

Hungarians rose up against Austrian rule, only to be crushed a few months later. On this day people gather outside the National Museum, where the revolution started, for speeches, recitals of poetry, and a rousing rendition of the National Anthem. Politicians tend to hijack the event, too, and the spirit of bullish nationalism that prevails today is possibly much the same as it was a century and a half ago.

August 20th is the saint's day of King Stephen, first Christian ruler of a united Hungary, crowned on Christmas Day 1000. Folk markets and fairs fill the town, and the event culminates in a magnificent fireworks display from Gellért Hill in the evening. Be warned: travelling across town becomes well-nigh impossible, as bridges are closed and public transport packed to bursting. It is best to make sure you are where you want to be well before the event.

October 23rd marks the beginning of the Hungarian uprising against Soviet rule in 1956. Workers, students and even members of the Hungarian army joined forces against Soviet tanks for a brief glorious 19 days, before Kádár made his pact with Khrushchev and the revolution was suppressed. The death-toll rose well into the thousands.

HISTORY

A lot of what you see in Budapest is newer than it appears. Classical and Gothic buildings are for the most part neo-Classical and neo-Gothic. Even the much-trumpeted Budapest Baroque was flourishing a good few decades later than the Baroque in many other European countries. This is, of course, a direct result of Budapest's turbulent history. Wave upon wave of occupation and subsequent destruction has taken its toll - and when each wave rolled on, it left surprisingly little in its wake.

The Romans were here. The Emperor Trajan established military and civilian townships at Aquincum, a little way north of what is now central Budapest. The Emperor Diocletian built a fortress on the Danube bank in the 3rd Century AD, near the present day Elisabeth Bridge. Magyar tribes did not actually enter the Carpathian Basin until the late 9th century, when Árpád led his people down from the Caucasus. The ruling House of Árpád was then established and continued to rule for three centuries.

One of its heirs, King - and later saint - Stephen (István), converted the people to Christianity and received a crown from Pope Sylvester II in 1000, which has since symbolised the independent Hungarian state and its adherence to Catholicism rather than the Orthodoxy of its Slav neighbours.

The principal settlement in early mediaeval times was Óbuda (the name means "old Buda") to the north of the inner city. But the Mongol invasion of 1241 prompted King Béla IV to move his court from the relative vulnerability of the flat Danube floodplain, up to Castle Hill. Buda and Pest were two completely separate towns, with Pest the site of trade and business while Buda was occasional home to the court and the treasury. During the early mediaeval period the court was semi-nomadic, moving around Transdanubia (the lands to the west of the Danube), and was not permanently based at Buda. By the 15th century, however, the Renaissance King Mátyás (Matthias Corvinus, 1443-1490) was so wealthy that he held court both at Visegrád, on the Danube Bend north of the city, and in Buda. Mátyás was celebrated as a paragon of cultured humanism. His

Count István Széchenyi by Tivadar Alconiere. Dubbed "the greatest Hungarian", Széchenyi's modernising zeal helped create the infrastructure that allowed Budapest to boom in the late 19th century.

palace at Buda is said to have rivalled anything in Europe for opulence and beauty, and visitors gasped at all the cloth of gold they saw, as well as at the ornamental gardens, fountains and statuary. Besides being home to every pleasure and luxury, the Hungarian court was also a centre of great learning. The famous *Biblioteca Corviniana*, which Mátyás founded, was kept on Castle Hill, and many scholars from all over Europe gathered in Buda as a result.

As so often happens with a strong monarch, his successors found him a hard act to follow. Struggles for the throne ensued, and, inevitably, disaster eventually struck. The boy king Lajos II was drowned in 1526 while retreating from the infamous Battle of Mohács (in southern Hungary), where the Hungarians were crushed by the Ottoman army led by Suleiman the Magnificent. Less than twenty years later the Ottomans had pushed west to Buda, which they overran in 1541. Hungary was then carved up into three parts with the Ottomans ruling the south and east to the Danube, Ferdinand Habsburg (brother of the Holy Roman Emperor Charles V) grabbing the north and west, and Transylvania (now part of Romania) becoming a vassal Ottoman state which was allowed a certain amount of internal political independence.

The Turks remained in Buda for 140 years. Period woodcuts show a city bristling with minarets - all have now vanished. Finally driven out in 1686 by the Habsburg armies of Leopold I, led by Eugene of Savoy and Charles of Lorraine, their few surviving relics include a

Sándor Petőfi, romantic poet and freedom fighter, who died in the struggle against Austrian domination in 1849.

PHOTO: BENCE KEPESSY / COURTESY OF THE HUNGARIAN NATIONAL MUSEUM

handful of Turkish baths and a small Muslim mausoleum on the slopes above Margaret Bridge.

After this followed a period of extensive rebuilding; this is the period of most of the Baroque buildings still extant today. The enlightened despotism of Maria Theresa (1717-1780) and her son Joseph II (1741-90) saw the growth of both Buda and Pest. Maria Theresa, realising the importance that Hungarian symbols of state had for the country, had Buda's Royal Palace rebuilt, returned the right hand of St. Stephen to Hungary (*see p. 72*) and ennobled many Hungarians - but it was Vienna that was the seat of power, and Hungarian affairs were controlled from Pressburg (now Bratislava); Buda was really no more than a provincial outpost of the Habsburg court.

It was not until the nineteenth century that the conception of a united Hungarian capital called Budapest really took off. In the first decades of the century the great reformer Count István Széchenyi undertook to shape the whole place up. Strongly Anglophile, he visited England repeatedly, and came back home full of schemes for steamships and railways on the English model. He also built the first permanent bridge over the Danube, and cut the tunnel through the Castle Hill. In 1848 the feverish spirit of nationalism which was coursing through Europe did not leave the city untouched. Anti-Habsburg feeling was stirred up on a political level by the fiery oratory of lawyer-turned-revolutionary Lajos Kossuth, and on a popular level by the idealistic young poet Sándor Petőfi. Kossuth declared an independent Hungarian capital in the eastern town of Debrecen, while Petőfi incited the masses to revolution with his inflammatory verses. Things went Hungary's way for a while - and then Austria called in the Russians to help them deal the recalcitrant Magyars a crushing blow. Hungary cocked a snook at Austria by surrendering not to the Kaiser but to the Czar. Austria tried to quell Hungary's rebellious spirit once and for all by ignominiously hanging as many of Hungary's generals as she could get her hands on. The country was desolate: Petőfi had been killed fighting, Kossuth had fled to Turkey and Count Lajos Batthyány, Prime Minister in Hungary's first independent government, faced the firing squad. It was only in 1867 that the wily old politician Ferenc Deák effected the so-called Compromise between the Habsburgs and the Hungarians. This allowed Hungary its own domestic government, but meant that foreign and military affairs were voted on jointly with Vienna. Under the system known as the Dual Monarchy, Emperor Franz Joseph was to remain Emperor in Austria, while in

Hungary he was crowned King. The Compromise Agreement effectively opened up the towns of Buda and Pest to foreign capital, and also opened the Austrian empire to Hungarian grain from the Great Plain, some of the most fertile arable land in Europe. The resulting explosion of wealth turned what had been two provincial little settlements on the banks of the Danube into a thrusting boomtown.

In 1873 Buda and Pest finally united to form a single capital city. After this came a period of rebuilding on a massive scale. Almost the whole of Pest was torn down, and its shabby, squat little buildings were replaced with glittering palaces and wide, tree-lined boulevards. Once described as the biggest village in Europe, the remodelled city now had to be seen to be believed. People started comparing it with Paris. In 1896 Budapest celebrated its "Millennium" - 1,000 years since the Magyar tribes first streamed into the Carpathian basin around 896. The people of Budapest were in confident, buoyant mood, and

The coronation of Franz Joseph as King of Hungary in 1867. His wife Elisabeth is wearing Hungarian dress. Beloved by Hungarians for her eager espousal of their cause, she was also accused by gossiping tongues of having an affair with Gyula Andrássy, Hungary's Prime Minister, who stands to the right of the dais.

PHOTO: ANDRÁS DABASI / COURTESY OF THE HUNGARIAN NATIONAL MUSEUM

they felt like an excuse for a massive party. "Now, at last, our true dawn is breaking," wrote one ecstatic historian, "The daystar of Hungary is about to shine in the European firmament."

The joy and optimism were not to last. At the Treaty of Trianon that followed the First World War, Hungary lost two thirds of her territory, and Budapest became the capital of a severely truncated country. This loss of territory at Trianon is still seen by the majority of Hungarians as the greatest tragedy that has befallen them at any time in their history. The 20th century was hard on Hungary. Budapest buildings still bear the bullet scars of its many bloody conflicts. The fall of the Habsburg empire was followed by the short-lived 1919 Republic of Councils or Commune, modelled on the Soviet prototype. It lasted barely a few brutal, triumphalist months before Admiral Horthy and his conservative regime suppressed it and took over. Horthy declared himself Regent (the theory being that he was ruling in place of the Habsburg King Karl IV, exiled in Madeira) and moved into the Royal Palace. Under his leadership a small élite enjoyed a graceful lifestyle, but it was not generally a prosperous time for Budapest. The grand city began to look a little dusty and down-at-heel.

The late thirties saw the introduction of restrictive Jewish laws. Though Hungary was a German ally in World War II, she tried to hold out against outright anti-semitism - but in 1944 the German army invaded. In October Horthy's government fell and was replaced by the Arrow Cross, an extreme nationalist movement which effectively capitulated to German Nazism and allowed the purges to be carried out. A Jewish ghetto was established in district VII, and the deportations began. In April 1945 the Red Army besieged Budapest. The German army retreated across the river, blowing up all the bridges behind them, and holed up on Castle Hill in Buda. The resulting siege left a smoking ruin of what had been a beautiful Baroque city, while Pest also suffered extensive bomb and shell damage.

The immediate post-war period, 1945-48, saw an attempt at democracy with multi-party elections and the re-formation of some pre-war parties. However, the cynical percentages agreement concluded between Churchill and Stalin, dividing Europe up into various spheres of interest, saw much of Eastern Europe being sacrificed to the Soviets in return for Greece. Hungary was supposedly divided 50-50 between Russia and the West, but it never happened. Mátyás Rákosi, "Stalin's best pupil", as he proudly called himself, insti-

tuted his "salami tactics", slicing up the social democrats and slinging "Fascist mud" at the right wing. He came to power on the back of rigged elections in 1948, ironically exactly 100 years since Russia had dealt Hungary her other mortal historical wound. Rákosi instigated one of the worst Stalinist regimes in the region, with the police terror, midnight arrests and show trials so well described by Arthur Koestler in *Darkness at Noon*.

After Stalin's death in 1953, the Soviet leadership was thrown into disarray and the Rákosi regime became increasingly anachronistic in the light of Khrushchev's more moderate style. Discontent began to be voiced in the country against Hungary's "little Stalin", and in October 1956, when a peaceful protest outside the Hungarian Radio headquarters was fired on by snipers, a full-scale uprising broke out against Soviet-style leadership. Communist moderate Imre Nagy was called on to lead the country towards Hungarian socialism. However János Kádár, who was initially on the side of the moderates, made a *volte-face* deal with the Russians. The Red Army entered the country in enormous numbers, arrested Nagy, who was later executed, and set Kádár at the head of a puppet government. Around a quarter of a million people left the country for good.

Kádár spent a few bloody years arresting and liquidating those involved, before making his famous "anyone who is not against us is with us" speech. His so-called Goulash Communism allowed a secondary economy to grow, with people working in the state sector by day and for themselves by night. Gorbachev, impressed by his record, once said that his *perestroika* had been partly inspired by the Hungarian model.

When in 1989 the Red Star was finally removed from the tip of the Parliament building Hungary, as a result of Kádár's measures, was not as paralysed by the emergence of a market economy as might have been expected. Budapest itself has changed with extraordinary speed over the last decade, and is now a bustling, prospering modern capital. Perhaps now, at long last, the predictions of those optimistic, excited turn-of-the-twentieth-century voices will come true: "Budapest will be a world metropolis, and crowds of people will flock from far and wide to see it".

A HANDFUL OF DATES

896 (approx.) The seven Magyar tribes arrive in the Carpathian Basin.

1000 Pope Sylvester II grants a crown to Stephen, first Christian monarch of Hungary.

1241 Invasion by the Mongols, who lay waste most of the country.

1541 Capture of Buda by the Ottomans.

1686 Expulsion of the Ottomans from Buda.

1848-9 Anti-Habsburg revolution, crushed by Austria, with the aid of Russia.

1867 Compromise Agreement between Hungary and Austria & Coronation of Franz Joseph as King of Hungary (as opposed to Emperor).

1919 Soviet-style Commune under Béla Kun.

1920 Treaty of Trianon deprives Hungary of two thirds of her territory.

1948 Hungary officially becomes a Communist state.

1956 Anti-Soviet uprising brutally crushed.

1989 Fall of Communism in Hungary.

A HANDFUL OF HEROES

Some of the famous figures from Hungarian history who occur and recur in this book:

GYULA ANDRÁSSY *(1823-1890)*

Hungary's Prime Minister after the Compromise Agreement with Austria. Handsome, dashing, fiercely patriotic but shrewd enough not to make Vienna his enemy, his government paved the way for the great boom years in Budapest.

LAJOS BATTHYÁNY *(1806-1849)*

First Prime Minister of Hungary after she declared herself independent of Austria in 1848. He was tried and executed by the Habsburgs.

FERENC DEÁK *(1803-1876)*

Wise and moderate politician largely responsible for engineering the Compromise agreement with Austria in 1867.

FRANZ JOSEPH *(reigned 1848-1916)*

King and Emperor, never a hero in Hungarian eyes, though his reign spanned much that has been crucial in Hungary's recent history, and saw Budapest's greatest period of glory - along with the inexorable decline of the empire to which it belonged.

LAJOS KOSSUTH *(1802-1894)*

Lawyer, journalist and nationalist who was a prime-mover in the anti-Habsburg struggle of 1848-9. After the Hungarian defeat he escaped into exile, dying in Italy.

SÁNDOR PETŐFI *(1823-1849)*

Romantic poet, born Alexander Petrovich to Slovakian parents in a town on the Great Plain. Fervent Hungarian freedom-fighter, author of a number of lyrics extolling love and freedom. He was killed fighting for the Hungarian cause.

ISTVÁN SZÉCHENYI *(1791-1860)*

Progressive-minded nobleman who played a large part in dragging Hungary from feudalism into the modern age. He built the Chain Bridge and the tunnel through Castle Hill, pioneered railways, the regulation of the course of the Danube, horse-racing, steamboats and much besides. Disillusioned and semi-insane, he committed suicide in Austria.

PART II

GUIDE TO THE CITY

Architecture

Theatrical and eclectic Budapest is one of the most architecturally beguiling cities in Europe. This is especially true of the architecture of Pest. The east side of the Danube is a triumph of town planning - almost all of what you see today was built between 1880 and the turn of the 20th century, in Historicist styles drawing from the Mediaeval, the Renaissance and the Baroque for their forms. And while the Second World War destroyed a large part of the city, especially alongside the river, many of the inner streets of Pest remain essentially unchanged. But building a whole city in twenty years obviously necessitated a few short cuts. At one point Budapest was developing faster than New York, and whole blocks went up seemingly overnight. The façades may all have looked stupendous, but scratch the surface, and you will see how stagey and flimsy the whole thing is. Huge blocks of what appear to be ashlar and rusticated masonry are in fact no more than cheap brick coated with wire and moulded plaster.

The Újszínház by Béla Lajta (1910).

The arrival of Secessionist architecture (Hungary's version of Art Nouveau) in the early 20th century only reinforced this stage-set impression, with its sinuous lines and emphasis on decoration. Between the wars Modernist influences began to make themselves felt - but even the starkest Hungarian buildings of the thirties cannot help but relieve the effect with some decorative motifs. After 1948, Socialist Realism laid its heavy ideological hand on architecture, but produced a lot of interesting buildings nevertheless. However, in the seventies, as the ideology began to run out of steam and modern architecture lost its spark, functional tower blocks mushroomed to meet burgeoning housing needs. Meanwhile, the architecture of past ages was allowed to crumble, and buildings that over the decades have been bombed, shot at and looted are now simply falling down. Restoration is beginning to happen, though, and new buildings are increasingly designed to complement their surroundings. Always remember to look upwards: the harsh glare of the shopfronts often belies a riot of gorgeous ornamentation on the first floor, all the more lovely for being slightly down-at-heel.

A Handful of Architects & Their Buildings

MIHÁLY POLLACK (1773-1855) - Born in Vienna, Pollack became a Pest citizen in 1802. He was a leading member of the Beautification Committee, set up in 1805 to develop the city, and therefore had a great architectural influence on the Hungarian capital. He was the architect of some of Budapest's finest Classicist buildings - of which few remain. The most famous is the National Museum (completed 1846, *see p. 103*). The house that he built for himself in 1822 still stands at József Attila utca No. 6, plain and unassuming but for the stonework above the door, modelled on the Palazzo Farnese in Rome.

MIKLÓS YBL (1814-1891) - When Ybl was buried in 1891, the funeral procession had to stop at numerous buildings all over the city in order to honour the man whose stamp was so firmly impressed on the face of the booming late 19th-century town. This great neo-Renaissance architect was responsible for many of Budapest's grandest buildings. It was he who designed the Opera House

(see p. 57), that symbol of civic and cosmopolitan pride - and undoubtedly his finest achievement, marking the rebirth of the Historicist style in Hungary by using Baroque elements in a mainly neo-Renaissance building. Constructed between 1875 and 1884, the period when opera houses were being built all over Europe, Ybl's building vies with them all for sheer refinement, and the foremost fresco-artists of the day were brought in to cover the interior from top to toe in Grecian allegory and *belle époque* fantasy. Ybl's style is reliably solid, symmetrical and elegant, but never startling. Some of his other famous designs include the Pumping Station on Ybl Miklós tér (now a casino and restaurant), as well as sections of the St. Stephen's Basilica (*see p. 71*) and the remodelling of the Royal Palace.

ÖDÖN LECHNER (1845-1914) - Famous for his declaration "There has never yet been a Hungarian language of form, but there will be", Lechner spent his life creating a Hungarian style that drew on folk motifs for its inspiration and that utilised Hungarian materials such as the majolica tiles produced by the Zsolnay firm. One of his best works

is the extraordinary Applied Arts Museum on Üllői út (*see p. 47*). Built between 1893-1896, it is a sort of cross between Moghul palace and Moorish Alhambra, all white icing-sugar arches within and majolica pinnacles without. The great glass roof that billows over the main hall creates a lovely, airy exhibition space. Other buildings by Lechner include the exuberant Postabank (*see*

The Applied Arts Museum, by Ödön Lechner.

p. 146) at Hold utca 4 (1900), the Thonet House at Váci utca 11/c (1890), adorned with pyrogranite and statuary, and, further afield, the Geological Institute at Stefánia út 14* (completed 1900), which has an enormous blue globe adorning the roof. Guided tours of the building are available on request. *Open 10am-4pm on Tuesdays and at weekends.*

GYŐZŐ CZIGLER (1850-1905) - Czigler was a professor of architectural design at the Budapest Technical University, but he also planned a number of well-known buildings around the city, evidencing a remarkable diversity of style. He designed No. 3 Andrássy út (*see p. 48*), and the neo-Baroque Széchenyi Baths (1913) in the Városliget (*see p. 27*). Perhaps his most interesting achievement, however, is the highly atmospheric Gozsdu udvar, built in 1904 (*see p. 154*). A series of seven apartment blocks connected by courtyards runs between Dob utca and Király utca in district VII. The courtyards were once occupied by artisans and craftsmen, who lived in the apartments above. Now everything is empty and rotting, but it is still interesting to walk through and watch how the light traverses the site, as well as to look into the forlorn, echoing, closed-up stairwells.

BÉLA LAJTA (1873-1920) - Lajta worked with Lechner during the first years of the 20th century, and initially he also drew extensively on folk forms. The strange conical domes he used in many of his mausoleums (which can be seen in the Jewish cemeteries on Kozma utca and Salgótarjáni utca*) are drawn from the *suba* or sheepskin cloak which shepherds wrapped themselves in to protect themselves from the bitter blizzards on the Great Plain. Lajta then moved away from the decorative forms of the early Art Nouveau to a cleaner, more Modernist approach. One such building is the Újszínház (New Theatre, 1910) at Paulay Ede utca 35 (*see p. 21*), where the use of hieratic geometric forms is very different from his design for the former Institute for the Blind (now a school) at Mexikói út 60*, built only a few years before - and where everything is designed to be felt rather than seen. Not far from the Újszínház, on Vas utca, is the Széchenyi School, where the vertical emphasis is broken only by abstract motifs. When it was built in 1912, one critic asked who were more fortunate, the pupils or the teachers, to attend such a model and well-designed school.

LÁSZLÓ VÁGÓ (1875-1933) - Started in architectural partnership with his brother József, and, like Lajta above, made the leap from Art Nouveau to Modernism. He built two houses on the experimental housing estate at Napraforgó utca*. The challenge was to build comfortable houses on a small site out in Buda on the banks of a deep ditch. Constructed in 1931, it was modelled on the Werkbund-Siedlung estate in Stuttgart and consisted of sixteen detached and three semi-detached houses with gardens. Twenty-two architects were involved in the project and, despite their various backgrounds, the whole development conveys a unity of purpose and vision. Although it is a bus ride out of town, anyone interested in Modernist architecture should take a look at it (bus No. 5 from Március 15. tér until the last stop at Pasaréti tér, from where it is a short walk).

KÁROLY KÓS (1883-1977) - Kós, like many architects of this period, was intent on creating a Hungarian style, but he looked to the middle ages for his inspiration. A devotee of John Ruskin and the Arts and Crafts Movement, he delved into the mediaeval folk past to create a new style. He was inspired by the village architecture of his native Transylvania, and employed its sloping roofs, steep gables and tiled turrets in much of his work. He designed several of the animal houses (1909-12) at the City Zoo at Állatkerti körút 6 (see p. 62), worth a visit for the architecture even if you can't bear seeing animals in cages. He also planned the centre of the Wekerle Estate*, a model housing estate for white-collar workers in the suburb of Kispest, built between 1912 and 1913.

1930s apartment block on Attila út.

LAJOS GÁDOROS (1910-1991) - Part of a post-World War Two designers' collective, Gádoros was one of the creators of the Parliamentary Offices on Széchenyi rakpart 19. Despite Tibor Fischer's send-up in his novel *Under the Frog* (Fischer maintains the architect had a hangover the morning he had to submit the design and used an old shoebox lying in his room to make the maquette), its plain white H-shaped bulk sits well next to the river. Built in 1948, as part of "the new spirit for new times" movement, it was formerly the Interior Ministry and much feared as a result. In 1949 Gádoros also built the Trade Union Headquarters (Dózsa György út 84/a), now being restored by Dutch architect Erik Van Egeraat. An amalgam of careful detail and simple mass forms, it is a good example of Hungarian post-war Modernist architecture.

IMRE MAKOVECZ (b. 1935) - Exponent of organic architecture, Makovecz - like so many of his early 20th-century predecessors - draws on ancient Hungarian folk motifs. One of his finest works is the mortuary chapel at the Farkasrét Cemetery (1977)*. An anthropomorphic work, with its ribbed ceiling and mysterious atmosphere, it is worth making the trip to see it. (Németvölgyi út 99). There is also a less successful office block at Szentkirályi utca 18, where he has added an organic structure to the top of a 19th-century building.

PÉTER REIMHOLZ (b. 1942) - Inspired by Japanese architecture as well as by Dutch Structuralism, Reimholz is concerned with space and motion. He creates elegant buildings that pay great attention to both exterior and interior detail, perhaps as a result of first studying product and interior design before qualifying as an architect. See his Hapimag timeshare apartment building at Fortuna utca 18 on Castle Hill, and his white brick apartment block at Logodi utca 44.

See Map References on p. 185 to locate these buildings.

Those marked with an asterisk require a full city map, available from bookshops.

BATHS

Not many years ago, one of the entries for the prestigious contemporary art award the Turner Prize was a video of the women's steam baths at the Gellért Hotel, Budapest. The idea would bring an amused smile to the face of most locals; what for them is an integral part of their city was for a British artist so extraordinary that it deserved to be transformed into a work of modern "art". Baths and Budapest are synonymous. The Romans first discovered that the area was rich in thermal springs; the mediaeval Hungarian kings developed them; but it was the Ottomans who really exploited Budapest's greatest natural resource. Islamic law decrees that a body should never be immersed in still water, and the traditional *hammam* has no pools of any kind. Here in Budapest, far from the *imams* of Constantinople, the Ottomans were able to indulge their love of water and sybaritic pleasures to the full. Fabulous domed baths with steam rooms, hot and cold pools and rest rooms sprang up along the Buda banks of the Danube. The only public baths in Pest, the Széchenyi, was not

Relaxing in the Gellért's indoor swimming pool.

built until the early 20th century, when thermal bathing had become a craze. Men who invested in the bathing complexes or bottling plants got rich on water as Budapest became a well-known spa. Today the city is again encouraging spa tourism - but you will still find that most of the baths are full of locals, swapping news and gossip in the steam.

NB: The opening times above are for the steam baths only; swimming pools in the same complex are usually open later at the weekends.

The list below is not exhaustive, but it covers the best and most central:

GELLÉRT - Art Nouveau baths studded in glazed tiles and mosaics. Part of the hotel of the same name, this huge complex was built in 1918 with separate baths for men and women and a communal indoor pool where middle-aged ladies in frilly bathing caps swim languidly round in circles. Large outdoor swimming pool with wave machine in summer. *Open Mon-Sun 6am-6pm. Buda XI, Kelenhegyi út 4.*

KIRÁLY - Built at the behest of Sokoli Mustapha Pasha in 1565, this is a well-preserved Turkish bath, complete with a domed bathing hall, hot and cold plunge pools and a chamomile-scented steam room. *Open for men Mon-Wed-Fri 9am-8pm; for women Tues-Thur-Sat 6.30am-6pm. Buda II, Fő utca 84. NB: On men's days the Király is mainly gay.*

LUKÁCS - Built in a neo-Classical style in the 19th century, the baths themselves are much older and were used by the Ottomans, to be extended into a spa complex much later. Set in a leafy courtyard next to the Institute for Rheumatology, there are numerous plaques all over the courtyard walls bearing thanks from visitors in many languages for the cures they received here. There are also two all-weather outdoor swimming pools, a whirlpool, sun terrace, and an old-fashioned marble drinking hall where you pay next to nothing for a beer mug of foul-tasting (but health-promoting) water. It's great fun, especially the whirlpool, which is so powerful that it literally sweeps you off your feet. All baths and pools are mixed. *Open Mon-Sat 6am-7pm and Sun 6am-5pm. Buda II, Frankel Leó út 25-29.*

RÁC - This is said to be the bath that the Renaissance King Mátyás visited by secret tunnels from his palace on Castle Hill. Today it is Turkish in its layout, but entirely rebuilt after

being flattened by bombs in 1945. It has none of the cavernous mystery of the Király or Rudas. Plans have been mooted to turn it into a hotel. *Open Mon-Sat 6.30am-6pm. For men Tues-Thur-Sat and for women Mon-Wed-Fri. Buda I, Hadnagy utca 8-10.*

RUDAS - A beautifully-preserved 400-year-old Turkish bath for men ONLY, with a separate swimming pool (for both sexes) which was added later. Specialises in massages. *Open Mon-Fri 6am-5pm, Sat-Sun 6am-1pm, last entry 12.00. Buda I, Döbrentei tér 9.*

SZÉCHENYI - This huge baths complex, the largest in Europe, was opened in the City Park (Városliget) in 1913. Neo-Baroque in style, it has an all-weather swimming area as well as steam rooms and hot pools. It is famous for its chess-players, who congregate around the chess boards at the edge of the large, steamy open-air pool. Both mixed and single-sex steam baths operate. *Open Mon-Sun 6am-7pm. Pest XIV, Állatkerti körút 11.*

Outdoor thermal water swimming pool at the Lukács Baths.

PRACTICAL TIPS

Choose which services you want from the list in the entrance and pay for them at the cash desk. You will get a separate receipt for each thing: mud bath, wet massage, dry massage etc. If you just want a steamy soak with no extras, a standard entry ticket is all you need.

You do not need to take towels to the Király or the Rudas, as you will be provided with a sheet to dry yourself at the end. Take towels to the others, and to all of them it is best to bring your own soap and shampoo (though you can buy it on site) and a pair of flip-flops. If the bath is single-sex, you need not wear a swimsuit unless modesty prevails. The exception here is the Király Baths, where swimsuits are supposedly compulsory, though most people take them off as soon as they get down to the hot pool. It's a good idea to have a T-shirt or hand towel with you to sit on in the steam room and sauna.

You will be given a cabin to change in and, in some of the baths, an extraordinary little apron to tie round yourself as you wander around. It won't cover much up, and you'll feel like something out of a *Carry On* film, but then so

Interior of the Széchenyi Baths.

does everyone. An attendant will lock the cabin and hand you a tag - take some small change with you for tips. If you're going to the Széchenyi or Gellért to use the swimming pool but not the steam, you will be given the choice of buying a ticket for a private changing cubicle or simply of taking a locker.

Most baths are arranged on a similar pattern: a central warm pool surrounded by steam room, sauna, hot pool and a deep cold plunge pool. There is a distinct bathing etiquette, which most of the older regulars follow: start with the dry sauna, shower, then plunge into the cool pool. Next, relax in the warm central pool until you are ready for the steam room, followed by the shock-to-the-system cold plunge pool. It's best to stay as still as possible in this, but some irrepressibles make it difficult by bouncing up and down, or even performing handstands. Rub yourself down if you want to use the dry sauna again - your body should not be wet when you enter. If you've paid for a massage, don't be daunted. The massage rooms often look a bit like something out of a Crimean War hospital - but though the masseuses seldom resemble Florence Nightingale, they do know how to loosen you up. Don't forget to tip him or her a couple of hundred forints afterwards. Drink plenty of water to rehydrate yourself when you finally finish.

To locate the baths, see Map References on p. 185.

THE CHAIN BRIDGE & ROOSEVELT TÉR

As the Eiffel Tower is to Paris and the Statue of Liberty is to New York, so the Chain Bridge is to Budapest: its quintessential symbol, stamped on all Hungarian hearts, and reproduced in thousands of souvenir keyrings, snowstorm paperweights and on the side of coffee mugs.

In December 1820 a young nobleman and officer, István Széchenyi, stationed on the eastern bank of the Danube, received news that his father had died in Vienna. At that time there was nothing but a pontoon bridge across the river which, because of the ice floes that hard winter, was not in use. Poor Széchenyi languished on the Pest river bank for a week before cannon fire announced the opening of the bridge. The incident led him to make a vow: to pay for a proper, fixed bridge whatever the cost. It took him nearly thirty years to do it; the Chain Bridge, designed by the Englishman William Tierney Clark and built by Scots engineer Adam Clark (no relation), was only officially opened in November 1849, just as the defiant Hungarian uprising against the Habsburgs was humiliatingly crushed. In a bitter twist of fate the first to go across the bridge was Baron Julius Jacob von Haynau, Commander-in-Chief of the Austrian army in Hungary, as he led his victorious troops into the Hungarian capital. And Széchenyi, after a severe nervous breakdown, was firmly installed behind the doors of the Döbling Mental Institution in Vienna, where he remained until he took his own life in 1860. Today the Széchenyi or Chain Bridge, the first permanent bridge in Budapest, is still the most magnificent bridge across the Danube.

The square into which the bridge flows on the Pest side of the river, Roosevelt tér, was once famed as the most perfect neo-Classical square in all Europe. It is far from being that now; instead it is best known for being the site of the Hungarian Academy of Sciences, the imposing dark honey-coloured building on the left as you come across the bridge. The academy was first founded by Széchenyi in 1825 – he is said to have donated an entire year's revenue to the project, and took rooms in the former Europa Hotel (the site is now occupied by the ugly modern building known as the "Spinach House" because of its lurid green colour) so that he could watch the construction work on its new Budapest headquarters from the windows of his suite. Széchenyi caused a sensation when the academy opened by making his inaugural speech in the vernacular Hungarian (a language he had assiduously learned; his first language was German) instead of Latin, which in those days was still the *lingua franca* of officialdom in the Habsburg empire.

Tucked behind the statue of Széchenyi in the centre of the square is a sorrowful-looking acacia tree, propped up on wooden stilts, reputedly the oldest tree in Budapest.

COFFEE HOUSES

Turn-of-the-century Budapest was known as "the town of 500 cafés". According to a late 19th-century tourist guide: "The Hungarian cannot do without the coffee house. On Sunday afternoons the space in the fashionable coffee houses seems too limited for the accommodation of the crowds which besiege them". It wasn't only the fashionable who used the coffee houses, though. Artists and writers who could not afford to heat their tiny attic flats used to have regular tables there, and would spend all day writing, smoking, making assignations and talking animated politics. Powdered ladies and moustachioed swells would eye each other up; aspiring poets wrote masterpieces on napkin corners. The best symbol of the Budapest coffee house, in its glory as well as its decline, is the New York at Erzsébet körút 9-11. Built in 1894 as a showcase for the New York Insurance Company, it is concocted in a spectacular glut of styles cased in marble, gilt and glass. From the start it was popular with a broad cultural set, from the bohemians to the nobility.

The popular Café Miró on Castle Hill, a touch of modernity amidst the Baroque.

Intellectuals and artists occupied their regular tables in the gallery alcoves while other visitors sat in the "deep end", the lower floor. One evening, to ensure that the café would never shut, the playwright Ferenc Molnár and friends threw its keys into the Danube. In those days the "writer's dish" was introduced: bread, cheese and cold cuts offered for a song, but only to writers. Regulars were even provided with pens and paper, and could sit for whole days, hardly spending a thing. The *maitre d'* during the period, Gyula Reisz, allowed endless credit to his chosen literary élite - he may not have had much of a head for business, but he should go down as one of the most faithful patrons of Hungarian literature! The café flourished until the First World War, enjoyed a brief revival in the thirties, and then went into decline. For by the thirties things were changing. "Modern youth is amazed by the idea that only a few years ago their parents used to spend their Sundays in the coffee house, uncomfortably attired in their very best clothes, in which they hardly dared to sit down," wrote Mrs Zsigmond Fülöp in 1933. In the 1950s the New York was turned into a sports shop. Today it is a coffee house again, waiting for its revival to happen. The crumbling building has been bought by developers - with luck they will restore it sensitively and keep it running. Traditional coffee houses all over the city have dwindled to only a handful, most of which have lost their genuine atmosphere, and rely largely on tourists for their clientèle. But Budapest's appetite for coffee is not dead, and a whole new breed of design-conscious cafés is springing up across town.

The Gerbeaud coffee house, the most famous in Budapest.

TRADITIONAL COFFEE HOUSES

ANGELIKA - Attempts have been made to get this former presbytery into the modern groove by filling it with whacky furniture and hanging modern art on the walls. Its weekday morning clientèle of elderly local ladies remains steadfastly loyal, however, and apart from their chatter the place is pleasantly subdued and peaceful. Cakes, coffee, salads and toasted sandwiches available, plus full meals in the glassed-in inner-courtyard restaurant section. A largish beer garden operates outside in summer. *Buda II, Batthyány tér 7.*

ASTORIA - The coffee is no more than acceptable, and the cakes are a bit of a let-down, but the décor and atmosphere more than make up for that. Fat marble pillars, palm trees and gilt-framed mirrors give it an air of graceful living. The card tables at the end of the room promise more of a saloon-bar feel, but are seldom occupied by hard-betting, hard-smoking poker players. Most of the time the place is genteelly placid, and the waiters so discreet it is often hard to attract their attention. *Pest V, Kossuth Lajos utca 19-21.*

BÉKE - Thirties-style coffee house in the Radisson Hotel. Serves some of the best cakes in town, and good coffee, which arrives in hand-painted Zsolnay porcelain. *Pest VI, Teréz körút 43.*

CENTRÁL - One of Budapest's classics, this place first opened in 1887 and by the 1890s had become a famous literary meeting place. The poet József Kiss (buried in the Jewish cemetery, *see p. 69*) held the editorial meetings of his daring new magazine *A Hét* (The Week) here every Friday and Saturday. After World War I the place was favoured by another periodical, *Nyugat* (West), which met here every Wednesday. Many of its writers immortalised the place in their works. This and other coffee houses frequented by intellectuals became famous as a hotline for news, gossip and the dissemination of ideas. The humorist Frigyes Karinthy once decided to measure how quickly it would take a joke to travel across the river. He told his joke in a coffee house in Buda, then an hour and a half later strolled into the Centrál, where the same joke was promptly told back to him. According to the novelist and playwright Ferenc Molnár, it was this phenomenal capacity for underground communication that made the coffee houses so unpopular with

Staff pose for the photo at the Ruszwurm in the 19th century.

the Communists: when they came to power in 1948, they had every coffee house in the city closed down. The Centrál reopened only a few years ago, and is once more the realm of dignified waiters in striped waistcoats serving dainty cups of coffee and thimblefuls of Magyar schnapps. *Pest V, Irányi utca 29.*

GERBEAUD - Famed in the last century for being the best and most elegant in town, this sumptuous place came into being as a result of a partnership between two patissiers: Henrik Kugler, a Hungarian, and Emil Gerbeaud, a Swiss, whom Kugler met in Paris. The

Gerbeaud's piano was originally intended for the Titanic - it saved itself from a watery grave by not being ready on time. The place's fame has meant that it is now a must-see on every tourist itinerary, and service can be frustratingly slow, while atmosphere is a bit lacking. But though it is no longer a place to go and linger for half an afternoon, and though the stylish octogenarian Hungarian ladies with their fur wraps and tangerine rinses have deserted it, it is definitely worth visiting for the décor. *Pest V, Vörösmarty tér 7.*

LUKÁCS - Once the coffee house of the Communist Police, set up in a

confiscated patrician mansion. Now restored, its twinkling chandeliers and lustrous Venetian looking-glass are the same as they always were, although the old regulars have never returned. The wall-to-wall carpet betrays Lukács's status as a 20th-century re-creation. *Pest VI, Andrássy út 70.*

Művész - Probably the best of the traditional places in terms of old-time atmosphere, though their plastic window stickers are a horrible mistake. It still attracts smoke-stained writers and ancient ladies in powder and pearls, and gives off a whiff of a vanished age. Its muted golds and greens and tarnished mirrors give it genuine appeal. *Pest VI, Andrássy út 29.*

Ruszwurm - The oldest café in the city (founded in 1827). It is tiny and cosy, furnished with marble and Biedermeier, non-smoking, and renowned for its pastries. The elderly lady in the picture (on the facing page) is Róza Ruszwurm, herself the daughter of a pastrycook who was imprisoned for his part in the 1848 uprising against Austria. In prison he met one of the commanders of the Hungarian forces, Rudolf Linzer, after whom he later named his Linzer biscuit: two rounds of short-cake sandwiched together with apricot jam and sprinkled with icing sugar. You can't always get Linzers in the Ruszwurm sadly, but they do still exist. *Buda I, Szentháromság utca 7.*

TRENDY CAFÉ-BARS

If you want to do as young Budapesters do, take yourself off to Liszt Ferenc tér. There is nothing remotely sedate or elegant about this place. Groups of boys and their dogs populate the centre of the square, aimlessly hanging around and provoking local residents to paroxysms of indignation about the dogshit and cigarette ends they leave behind them. In the meanwhile the rest of the square has become café-land *par excellence*, catering to a young and image-conscious crowd, with outdoor tables multiplying under the trees in summer. The Music Academy at the far end provides musical accompaniment as students practise madly for exams: broken chords and difficult chromatic scales compete with the boom-boom beats emanating from the bars down below. The cafés that line the square - Vian, Incognito, Pesti Est Café and the

Café Vian, one of the new-look cafés in town.

Fashion Café nearby on Andrássy út, along with the Café Miró up on Castle Hill in Buda - are intensely style-aware, and derivative rather than quintessential Hungary. You might not feel at home here without your mobile phone. Film and TV personalities, fashion designers, coiffeurs, night club owners, models - all have been spotted here.

OLD-STYLE CAFÉS

Before the Iron Curtain came down, the *cukrászda* (pastry shop) and the *presszó* (coffee bar) were real Budapest institutions, to be found on every street corner, the floors tiled with mosaic-look tile fragments, the tables covered with plastic lace-look cloths, and a pall of cigarette smoke hanging in the air. Coffee would be served in a glass on a saucer, with a cheap aluminium spoon and two lumps of sugar. Now most places go in for cappuccino. But there are a few survivors:

BAMBI PRESSZÓ - This place even has a concrete terrace where you can sit out with a beer in summer. The omelettes are quite decent. Inside, men congregate to play speed chess or dominoes, and sometimes throw the pieces around when things aren't going their way. I don't think a breath of fresh air has blown through the room since it opened, but it retains a faithful following. *Buda II, Frankel Leó út 2.*

IBOLYA PRESSZÓ - The difference between a *cukrászda* and a *presszó* is that *presszós* serve beer and spirits, and as a natural consequence tend to be smokier. Here the beer is real Hungarian, from the southern town of Pécs, and it occurs to no one that bleeping games machines might lower the tone. *Pest V, Ferenciek tere 5.*

NO. 1 - If you want a place whose atmosphere will whirl you straight back to the early seventies, look no further. The décor and furniture certainly haven't changed since then - and by the look of them neither have many of the customers. The bar offers "coctails", but you are probably safer sticking to beer. Do as the locals do and drink a flagon of it with a tiny glass of *pálinka* (fruit brandy) as a chaser. *Pest V, Sas utca 9.*

SZALAI CUKRÁSZDA - Bitter coffee in a glass and award-winning cakes. Hot chocolate available in winter, ice creams in summer. Three large, gilt-framed mirrors vie with three bright red lampshades, the sort of thing you might have made in craft class at school. *Open every day except Tuesday. Pest V, Balassi Bálint utca 7.*

HUNGARIAN CAKES & PASTRIES

Count István Széchenyi once remarked that: "Things are only going well in a country if the tailor, the soap-maker and the patissier are firmly convinced that the happiness of the nation depends on their skill".

As far as cakes are concerned, his opinion still stands. Cakes are a vital part of Hungarian life. Late on Sunday mornings the streets in residential areas will be deserted except for a steady file of people carrying home beautifully-wrapped pastries from the corner *cukrászda*. Here are a few of the best:

DOBOS TORTA: A rich confection of chocolate sponge and chocolate cream filling, topped with crunchy caramel.

FRANCIA KRÉMES: A puff pastry base crowned with a vast wadge of light vanilla cream and topped with sticky caramel.

ESTERHÁZY TORTA: A delicious soft cake, made of layered ground walnuts and vanilla cream (*see picture overleaf*).

GERBEAUD (OR ZSERBÓ) SZELET: A sticky layered slice made of chocolate, jam and ground walnuts.

ISCHLER: Two round shortcake biscuits sandwiched together with jam and coated in melted chocolate.

POGÁCSA: A savoury scone, made either with cheese (*sajtos*), or pork cracklings (*tepertős*), and sometimes with potato (*burgonyás*).

RÉTES: This is the Magyar name for what the Austrians call *strudel* - and Hungary claims to have invented it. It typically comes with apple and cinnamon, poppy-seed, sour cherry, or sweet curd cheese fillings.

RIGÓ JANCSI: A chocolate and vanilla sponge square filled with chocolate fondant. It is named after a famous 19th-century violinist who eloped with French countess.

TÚRÓS TÁSKA: A puff pastry shell filled with sweet curd cheese and raisins.

TYPES OF COFFEE

CAPPUCCINO: Gone are the days when Hungarian cappuccino was lukewarm Nescafé topped by a glob of fake cream from an aerosol and sprinkled with hundreds and thousands. Now you can order one and breathe easy.

TEJES KÁVÉ (OR MÉLANGE): Espresso coffee with milk. Sometimes it comes ready mixed, sometimes the milk comes in a separate jug.

PRESSZÓ KÁVÉ: A small shot of black coffee (if you want a longer shot, ask for a *dupla*). If you just order a "coffee", without specifying what kind, this is what you will get.

HOSSZÚ KÁVÉ: Espresso coffee made weaker with the addition of more water - but not as weak as an American coffee. Specify whether you want it with milk or not; and if you want the milk to be hot, then it is always worth saying so.

MUSEUMS & GALLERIES

Budapest is generously endowed with art galleries. And though a lot of artists like to complain about how tough the censorship years of Communism were, the fact is that the sector was generously subsidised (provided you toed the line, of course), and artists enjoyed a large amount of respect. The form of address *Művész úr* (Mr Artist) is still used today. This favoured status has helped to create a few problems though: too many small galleries, not enough good art, and too few really good exhibitions. And underfunding is also now playing its part. In the larger national galleries and exhibition halls, genuine masterpieces are mixed in alongside genuine dross, the lighting and hanging are not always very well done, and whole rooms are sometimes closed because of staff shortages. There are lovely things to see, however, and knowing exactly what you are looking for makes it much easier.

Poppy Seed Cake (1910) by Adolf Fényes, a number of whose folk-genre paintings can be seen in the Hungarian National Gallery.

Unless otherwise stated, opening times are Tues-Sun 10am-6pm (April-Sept) and 10am-5pm (Oct-March). Closed Mon. Last tickets 30 minutes to 1 hour before closing.

HUNGARIAN NATIONAL GALLERY

Taking up the main wing of the former Royal Palace, the collections here allow the viewer a good look at Hungarian art over the ages. The beauty of *The Visitation* (1506, in the mediaeval collection), once part of an altar, with its exquisite combination of human figures, landscape elements and wild flowers, will stun those who thought that late mediaeval art stopped at the Alps. Much 19th-century history painting is on an epic scale, but Munkácsy, with his enormous tarred canvases, has a truly individual voice, and the whimsical creations of Károly Lotz have genuine charm and appeal. Pál Szinyei Merse is the best-known voice of the Hungarian pastoral idyll, but perhaps the styles which were to find most resonance in Hungary were Art Nouveau and Symbolism. János Vaszary's dream-like canvases, Rippl-Rónai's wistful portraits, or Gulácsy's ghostly visions, all on the second floor, are supreme examples

of this period. A refreshing counter to this indulgent world are the folk-genre works of Adolf Fényes, particularly his *Poppy Seed Cake* (1910). Maverick painter Tivadar Csontváry, whom Picasso recognised as a fellow genius at the beginning of the 20th century, dominates the second floor landing with his huge canvas of the Greek theatre at Taormina. Many of the works on the top floor seem like imitations of French isms and trends, but don't overlook István Farkas' *Madman of Syracuse*, some say one of the best 20th-century paintings in the building. *Buda I, Budavári Palota, buildings B, C, D.*

PAINTERS TO LOOK OUT FOR IN THE NATIONAL GALLERY

First Floor

KÁROLY LOTZ (1830-1904) - Lotz perhaps contributed more to the 19th-century face of the city than any other painter then or since. His romantic Historicist style (also adopted by his contemporaries Bertalan Székely and Gyula Benczúr) can be found in frescoes in the Opera House and Parliament, as well as in countless villas around town. One of the most striking is the Art Nouveau-fronted department store

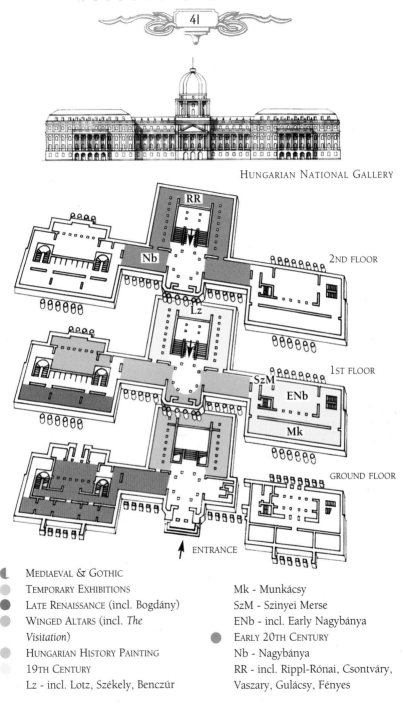

HUNGARIAN NATIONAL GALLERY

RR

Nb

2ND FLOOR

Lz

SzM

ENb

1ST FLOOR

Mk

GROUND FLOOR

ENTRANCE

MEDIAEVAL & GOTHIC

TEMPORARY EXHIBITIONS

LATE RENAISSANCE (incl. Bogdány)

WINGED ALTARS (incl. *The Visitation*)

HUNGARIAN HISTORY PAINTING

19TH CENTURY
Lz - incl. Lotz, Székely, Benczúr

Mk - Munkácsy

SzM - Szinyei Merse

ENb - incl. Early Nagybánya

EARLY 20TH CENTURY
Nb - Nagybánya

RR - incl. Rippl-Rónai, Csontváry, Vaszary, Gulácsy, Fényes

at Andrássy út 37, where, on the first-floor, the "Lotz Room" still survives, former salon of the gentlemen's club that used to occupy the building. Lotz was the public artist *par excellence*, and a range of his paintings are on display in the gallery.

MIHÁLY MUNKÁCSY (1844-1900) - A poor peasant boy from a village now in the Ukraine, Munkácsy went on to fame and riches in Paris, and even married a Belgian baron's widow. It is definitely his early pictures, filled with suffering and doubt, that are worth looking at. Acclaimed in his lifetime as the greatest Hungarian artist (after his death his body lay in state on a ceremonial bier in Heroes' Square for all to pay homage to), Munkácsy's success turned him into rather a vain man. Wanamaker, the US department-store tycoon, bought his *Christ Before Pilate* for a fantastic sum. But Paris and the salons ruined him with their easy money and elegant ways. He contracted syphilis at an early age, which contributed to his brooding outlook. Sadly he mixed bitumen with his paint and his canvases are getting darker and darker as a result - and nothing can be done about it.

Golden Age (1898), by János Vaszary.

Second Floor

TIVADAR KOSZTKA CSONTVÁRY
(1853-1919) - This strange man,
who started life as a pharmacist and
only turned to art after a vision
which he had in his twenties, is
enormously popular today, though
he was wholly unrecognised in his
own lifetime. He travelled extensively in the Balkans and the Holy Land,
working furiously at huge, searing
canvases. His work may be a bit
naive for some; others revel in the
way he was totally unafraid to use
colour. His huge canvas of the Greek
theatre at Taormina hangs on the
2nd floor landing, while other works
hang in the gallery to the right of the
stairs (*see plan on p. 41*).

LAJOS GULÁCSY (1882-1932) -
Gulácsy was subject to Symbolist
visions and created his own fantasy
world of Na'Conxypan, peopled
with the strange, phantom-like figures you can see in his dreamy,
deceptively innocent, subtly disturb-
ing works. He even compiled a
dictionary of Na'Conxypan words,
writing poems into his text about
this wraith-like land in a language
only he could decipher. He spent the
last thirteen years of his life entirely
in psychiatric hospitals suffering
from severe schizophrenia.

NAGYBÁNYA SCHOOL - The rural landscapes of Nagybánya in Transylvania
(now Baia Mare, Romania) inspired a
whole school of painting at the turn
of the century. *Plein-air* artists
flocked to what became a well-
known colony to produce their own
version of Impressionism, and the
painter Simon Hollósy transferred
his art school from Munich to
Nagybánya in 1896. As in France,
the painters were reacting against the
prevailing Historicist and salon-
painting styles, but in Nagybánya
they were also seeking a Hungarian
mode of expression. Folk motifs and
a use of colour which was almost
Gauguinesque in its daring bright-
ness became popular. Painters to
look out for include Károly
Ferenczy, who soaks his canvases in
sunlight, or Oszkár Glatz, who con-
sciously used folk themes in his
work. Some of the works will seem
derivative, but Ferenczy's *October* or
Sunny Morning (1905) and Glatz's
Boys Wrestling (1901) stand on their
own as great works of art. The
Nagybánya colony operated until the
mid 1930s.

JÓZSEF RIPPL-RÓNAI (1861-1927) -
Hailed as the Father of Hungarian Art
Nouveau, he was at once painter,
draughtsman and applied artist. As
part of the Nabis group in France he

knew Bonnard and Bernard, but his use of flat colour and clear lines was more for decorative purposes than impressionistic ones. His huge body of work covers everything from tea-sets to tapestries, but perhaps his greatest works are the small-town interiors and garden scenes, and inti-mate portraits of the people he loved, his family, lovers and relations.

JÁNOS VASZARY (1867-1939) - Vaszary's work *Golden Age* (1898) is one of the great symbolist Hungarian works of art. Lovers occupy a nar-cotic gilded world, where spirits float in the autumnal smoke. In the twenties Vaszary went on to paint fast city scenes, one of which can be seen on the third floor, but his finest work was executed at the turn of the century, when the Budapest boom produced some of its greatest works of art and literature.

Top Floor

ISTVÁN FARKAS (1887-1944) - Born into a well-to-do Jewish family, Farkas lived in Paris in the 1910s, meeting and impressing Apollinaire and living next door to Rilke. Thrown out of France as an enemy alien at the beginning of World War I, he worked as a war artist on the front, returning to Hungary in 1919 after a short spell in an Italian prisoner-of-war camp. During the inter-war years his work became increasingly tense and dis-turbing, and as the Hungarian Jewish laws began to take effect from 1937, his life became ever more con-strained. He was well-enough con-nected to have been able to hide or even escape, but in his last recorded

Fate, one of the sinisterly atmospheric works by István Farkas in the National Gallery.

message, in June 1944, he declared that "if human dignity is so debased, then it is no longer worth living". He was murdered in Auschwitz.

LUDWIG MUSEUM

Founded by German chocolate millionaire Peter Ludwig, this museum is also found in the Royal Palace, in Building A. Apart from a reasonable collection of contemporary Hungarian works, it is also the place to look for interesting temporary shows - Cindy Sherman, Josef Beuys and Brassaï have all been shown there in recent years.

NATIONAL MUSEUM

Permanent exhibition covering Hungarian history from the conquest until 1990. The 20th century is particularly well done, with great 1919 republic posters and archive footage, a Second World War bunker, and a fifties TV set showing endless speeches by János Kádár. Housed in a lovely neo-Classical building which is currently being restored.

ETHNOGRAPHIC MUSEUM

Once the Constitutional Court building, this magnificent pile right oppo-

October, by Károlyi Ferenczy, a member of the Nagybánya School active from the late 19th century to the late 1930s.

site Parliament is well worth visiting for its entrance hall alone. It is famously unsuited to its present role - locals maintain that it is only really any good as a film set (it was used repeatedly in Alan Parker's *Evita*) - and when you see its marble stairs and frescoed ceilings you will see what they mean.

FINE ARTS MUSEUM

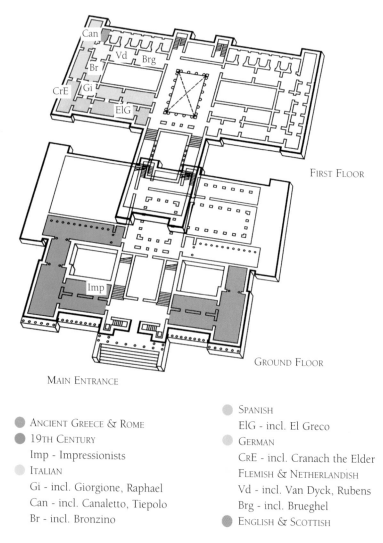

FIRST FLOOR

GROUND FLOOR

MAIN ENTRANCE

● ANCIENT GREECE & ROME
● 19TH CENTURY
  Imp - Impressionists
○ ITALIAN
  Gi - incl. Giorgione, Raphael
  Can - incl. Canaletto, Tiepolo
  Br - incl. Bronzino

○ SPANISH
  ElG - incl. El Greco
○ GERMAN
  CrE - incl. Cranach the Elder
  FLEMISH & NETHERLANDISH
  Vd - incl. Van Dyck, Rubens
  Brg - incl. Brueghel
● ENGLISH & SCOTTISH

Upstairs is a permanent exhibition on Hungarian peasant life and folk traditions with some marvellous and memorable photographs. *Pest V, Kossuth tér 12.*

FINE ARTS MUSEUM

Housed in an austerely grand building, its main hall massive and imposing like a Victorian railway station, this gallery boasts one of the best collections of Spanish art outside Spain: a total of seven El Grecos are to be found in the left-hand wing on the first floor. Other works to look out for include a fantastically erotic Bronzino (*Venus, Cupid and Jealousy*), a Raphael (the *Esterházy Madonna*), and two Giorgiones - rare because very little of his work survives anywhere. There is also an excellent Netherlandish collection containing some truly lovely pieces, including a superb Brueghel. Overall the museum's collection gives the impression of having been deliberately and painstakingly put together, with every major artist represented by at least one work (Van Gogh seems to be a notable exception to this rule), even if not always a great or characteristic one. The result is that the museum works brilliantly as a lightning, teach-yourself tour of European history of art. *Pest XIV, Hősök tere. Open Tues-Sun 10am-5.30pm. Closed Mon.*

APPLIED ARTS MUSEUM

Perhaps the most fantastic building of all, this fabulous concoction was designed by Ödön Lechner (*see p. 21*). Inside it offers ceramics, carpets, clothes and metalwork. A far-sighted collections policy in the early 20th century meant that a lot of Art Nouveau masterpieces were bought at the 1900 Paris exhibition. Presentation is not sophisticated, but this needn't matter: the objects speak for themselves. *Pest IX, Üllői út 33-37. Open Tues-Sun 10am-4pm. Closed Mon.*

RÓTH MIKSA MUSEUM

A little museum dedicated to the work of glass painter and mosaicist Miksa Róth (1865-1944). Responsible for much of the turn-of-the-century stained glass in the city (Postal Museum, Parliament, Music Academy, Agricultural Museum), Róth used glass like paint, creating sinuous designs in luminous colours with techniques to rival Tiffany. His former home now houses a small collection of his work, with some rooms reconstructed in the heavy pre-Raphaelite style so beloved at the time, with items of Róth's original furniture and belongings.
Budapest VII, Nefelejcs utca 26. Open Tues-Sun 2pm-6pm.

POSTAL MUSEUM

Housed in what was once a sumptuous town residence. The metal template initials of the owner, Andreas Saxlehner, and his wife (AS and ES) can still be seen on the street door. The entranceway is splendid, decorated with frescoes by Károly Lotz, the foremost fresco artist of his age. The Saxlehner wealth came from bottled mineral water, and tribute is paid to that noble trade by the friezes in the entranceway. One shows the god Mercury dispatching bottles to earth to cure mortal ills, another shows a sick man having the water administered to him, and a third shows nubile women bathing in it. The Postal Museum, upstairs on the first floor, is housed in what used to be the old Saxlehner apartment. The wooden fittings, English silk wallpaper and Murano crystal chandeliers are all the originals, and the cameo female heads on the ceiling of the main salon are said to be portraits of Saxlehner's opera-singer wife Emma. *Budapest VI, Andrássy út 3 (Press "10" on the bell panel to be let in). Open Tues-Sun 10am-4pm.*

ÁVH 56 MUSEUM

A museum dedicated to those who perished in the 1956 revolution is soon to open in the former ÁVH headquarters, a building where, in the words of novelist and essayist Sándor Márai, "any cruelty that the human mind could invent was perpetrated". The ÁVH (State Security Authority) operated as the Hungarian equivalent of the KGB in the fifties, extracting "confessions" and sentencing people to their deaths - often for crimes that they and their torturers knew full well they hadn't committed. Even Communist party members were not safe; János Kádár himself was a victim of ÁVH cruelty, before his "rehabilitation" in 1954. The ÁVH came to be so hated that during the 1956 uprising a crowd stormed the building, captured anyone working inside and lynched them on the spot. The plaque on the outside wall reads: "Though you may forgive the murderers, never forget the horror of the terror, and remember the victims". *Pest VI, Andrássy út 60. At the time of going to press the Museum was not yet open.*

STATUE PARK

After the collapse of Communism in 1989, Budapest began gleefully toppling its sculpted Lenins and Stalins from their cast iron and marble

perches. Realising that an episode of history was fast being rubbed out, two enterprising young Hungarians decided to set up a museum dedicated to all this discredited Communist iconography. The result is the Statue Park (*Szoborpark*), were you will find Marxes, Lenins and Engelses aplenty, as well as Hungarian Communist leaders, all in fine Socialist Realist style. The park is well laid out, and also boasts a tongue-in-cheek shop where you can buy "Molotov Cocktails" and CDs of rousing proletarian songs. Although it is a bit of a trek, it is well worth a visit (best to take a taxi, though public transport also works: bus No. 3 from Buda XI, Karinthy Frigyes út, and then bus No. 50 from Jókai Mór utca to the last stop). Gyula Illyés' famous poem, *One Sentence on Tyranny*, is beaten onto the huge gates. "Where there is tyranny, Everyone is a link in the chain." *Szobor Park, Buda XXII, on the corner of Balatoni út and Szabadkai út. Open 10am-7pm every day.*

See Map References on page 185 to locate museums and galleries.

Marx and Engels, two of the fallen idols now exiled to the Statue Park.

Some Nobel Prizewinners

Albert Szent-Györgyi

(1893-1986) - Chemist who discovered Vitamin C. He writes that sometime in 1932 his wife gave him some bread and butter and green paprika for tea, but instead of eating the paprika he whisked it away to the lab. He found it to contain massive amounts of Vitamin C or hexuron acid, which he had been trying to isolate for some time. He was awarded the prize in 1937.

Jenő Wigner

(1902-1995) - Physicist who received the prize in 1963 for the proposal and application of the modern symmetry-based theory of fundamental physical forces. He was one of those who, in 1939, drew Albert Einstein's attention to the fact that the Germans might use atomic energy for military purposes. This resulted in the Manhattan Plan, which allowed for the development of the atomic bomb, something that sorely distressed Wigner until the end of his life.

Dénes Gábor

(1900-1979) - Physicist whose interest in electron-optics led him to discover the holograph. He realised in the late forties - twenty years before the invention of the laser - that information not only about the intensity of refracted light waves but also about their phases must be employed to create a complete (holo) and spatial image (graph).

György Békésy

(1899-1972) - Physicist who won the prize in 1961 for his work on human hearing, particularly for his discovery of the stimulus mechanism found in the cochlea. For his research he needed to dissect a great number of heads. He once remarked that he was grateful to many people, especially to the police officer who informed him in retrospect that he could have been arrested at any time on suspicion of murder, given that he carried human heads about in his briefcase.

MUSIC

Hungary is famed for a musical tradition that has always diverged from the European mainstream. It has also produced one of the undisputed geniuses of 20th-century classical music: Béla Bartók (1881-1945). His musical achievement went far beyond being simply an achievement for his own homeland; he had a profound influence on the whole of 20th-century music. One of his chief sources of inspiration was the folk music of Hungary, and he travelled around the country making field recordings of village musicians. The most perfect expression of his restless, questing, yet curiously light, resolved and intimate style are probably the string quartets, pieces which go some way towards fusing the verve of Stravinsky, the brittle tension of Debussy and the homely cadences of folk song. Yet for all his love for his country, when the Jewish laws were introduced he wrote a public letter expressing his disgust and sadness that Hungary was capable of such infamy, and left the country in 1940, despairing at the rise of Fascism. He emigrated to New York and never returned to Europe again.

Inside the Opera House, Hungary's greatest neo-Renaissance building.

Zoltán Kodály partnered Bartók in the collection of folk songs. His output includes the rousing *Psalmus Hungaricus* and *Budavári Te Deum* (the first was composed to celebrate the 50th anniversary of the union of Buda and Pest; the second to commemorate the 250th anniversary of the Turkish surrender of Buda Castle). But he is best known as a great pedagogue, developer of the famous "Kodály Method" of music teaching.

Apart from classical music, Hungary is also one of the foremost folk music nations of the world, with a tradition which, if not quite living, definitely exists within living memory. The style of the music, based on its own peculiar pentatonic scale, is instantly recognisable after you have heard it once, and it has had a penetrating influence on the folk traditions of neighbour nations such as Romania. The Dance House Movement of the 1970s aimed with some success to re-establish the prominent place of folk music in people's consciousnesses. Today the success of folk singer Márta Sebestyén - whose voice appears in the films *The English Patient* and *Flirt* - has brought Hungarian folk to an interna-

The interior of the Liszt Music Academy. On the right hand side is Aladár Körösfői-Kriesch's mosaic Fountain of the Muses. Körösfői-Kriesch was a prominent member of the Hungarian Arts and Crafts movement in the early 20th century.

tional audience, although she is less famous at home, and as the folk revival runs out of steam somewhat, there are few new voices coming up behind her.

Then there are the *nóta*, popular 19th-century tunes, usually either sorrowful love ditties or merry drinking songs, which were quickly picked up by the Roma (gipsy) violinists who played to guests - and still do - in Budapest restaurants. This is not traditional gipsy music, however, nor is it strictly folk music, though it was not until Kodály and Bartók set off round the country to collect folk songs with their primitive recording equipment that the difference was fully realised. *Nóta* are essentially a 19th-century urban invention, but to many city-dwellers they represented real Magyar music, and as a result deserve a mention, even if music purists don't consider them the real thing.

WHO TO LOOK OUT FOR AND WHERE TO GO

CLASSICAL MUSIC

Symbol of Budapest's classical music scene *par excellence* is the Liszt Academy. This Art Nouveau concert hall on the corner of Király utca and Liszt Ferenc tér (built in 1907) is one of the great musical venues of the world. The exterior is square-built and sober, giving no hint at all of what lies within. The reason for this oyster-shell approach is because government pressure forced the architects Korb and Giergl to shift from their original Art Nouveau designs to the neo-Baroque which the Emperor Franz Joseph so loved. However, the government watchdogs looked no closer than the exterior façades. The interior shimmers in green and gold and is one of the Art Nouveau masterpieces of the city. Frescoes, mosaics and stained glass by leading masters adorn the concert hall and its foyers. The hall itself has erotic quasi-Nubian girls holding up the roof, and the ceiling is covered in golden leaves. As an institute the Liszt Academy is Budapest's premier centre of music teaching and has turned out some great conductors, including Sir George Solti. In its heyday it had Bartók teaching piano and Kodály teaching composition. And although the teaching side of the Academy has fallen, it still attracts its fair share of top-class performers. A good concert here is an experience not to be missed. The best native Budapest orchestras are the Budapest Festival Orchestra, the Nemzeti Philharmónia and the Hungarian Radio and TV Orchestra. Performers to look out for are pianists Dezső Ránki and András Schiff (at the very top of the league; Schiff no longer lives in the country), with Zoltán Kocsis and Jenő Jandó in second division. Other names are cellist Miklós Perényi, organist Xaver Varnus, and vocal group Capella Savaria, who specialise in the Baroque. There is also the mellow-voiced baritone László Polgár - catch him if you have the chance, as he now rarely performs at home in Hungary.

FOLK MUSIC

The best group around is probably Muzsikás, who play on Thursday nights in the leisure centre on Marcibányi tér - at least they do if they aren't on tour. Since the international success of folk singer Márta Sebestyén - whom they accompany - with Deep Forest and in *The English Patient*, the group are in much more demand outside Hungary, and in fact she and Muzsikás are more likely to pack a concert hall in London or New York than in Budapest. If you can't get to see them on their home turf, plenty of

their music is available on CD, both with and without Sebestyén.

If you want to listen to live folk, the best place is the Fonó*, out in district XI at Sztregova utca 3, which hosts folk music from all over the globe, though predominantly from the Balkans and Carpathian Basin. Frequent concerts and folk festivals are held in the leisure centre on Almássy tér, too; check the publications listed on p. 174 for information about what's on. Fonó also have their

Contemporary composer György Kurtág.

own record label, and their album collection includes a lot of folk and gipsy music from the Eastern European region, including the *Új Pátria* recordings of still-surviving Hungarian folk musicians, mainly from Transylvania. Fonó CDs are available from the concert house itself, as well as in major outlets around town.

NÓTA

Nóta are becoming harder to find, since gipsy bands in restaurants play more and more international evergreens and fewer and fewer *nóta*. However, you can always ask. If the musicians approach your table and invite requests, try them with *Nincsen rózsa tövis nélkül* (There are no roses without thorns) or *Lakodalom van a mi utcánkban* (There's a wedding in our street). They are sure to know those. If you do encourage the musicians to play at your table, it is customary to tip them afterwards. If you develop a real taste for *nóta*, the best place to go is the Rézkakas restaurant on Veres Pálné utca in district V, where Róbert Kúti and his band are on hand to get your toes tapping under the table.

ROMA MUSIC

Real Roma music is by turns mournful and wild. Using the most basic instruments, like the washboard, the milkchurn and spoons, groups turn out extraordinarily evocative and moving music, often bewailing the fate of an ethnic minority much-beleaguered in this part of Europe. The two most popular bands, both of whom give fairly frequent concerts, are Ando Drom (On the Way) and Kalyi Jag (Black Fire). Both groups hail from Budapest and sing both in Romany and in Hungarian. Recordings by both groups are also widely available on CD. Representing the modern strand of the genre are Fekete Vonat (Black Train), named after the train that runs from the eastern part of Hungary, carrying Roma workers to jobs in the city. This Roma Rap outfit, with the glorious Fatima as lead vocalist, sings about Budapest's district VIII, which has a reputation as a Roma ghetto.

CONTEMPORARY MUSIC & JAZZ

György Kurtág (1926 -) is probably Hungary's best and certainly its most famous living composer. He began his musical career at Budapest's Liszt Academy in 1946 under Sándor Veress and Leó Weiner, and then from 1957-8 he studied under Darius Milhaud and Olivier Messiaen in

Paris. His atonal, difficult work is grounded in Bartók and Webern. He has collaborated a lot with Hungarian soprano Adrienne Csengery, often drawing on fragments of poems or literary works for his musical texts.

Other names to look out for include Tibor Szemző, founder-member of the percussion ensemble the 180 Group (so called as 180 cm was the average height of its fifteen members) which premiered the work of composers such as Steve Reich in Hungary. His marvellous *Tractatus* is based on the philosophical hypotheses of Wittgenstein: while the text is read in three or four different languages, Szemző hums a melody underneath. Jazz pianist György Szabados describes himself as an "avant-garde from the Pilis Hills" and, like a true post-modern, is already thinking about how the things he does will sound in his memoirs. His piano-and-chanting composition *Revelation* (*Jelenés*), with Canadian saxophonist Roscoe Mitchell, is Szabados at his lunatic best. Folk-inspired jazz saxophonist Mihály Dresch founded a quartet which originally included the folk violin maestro Félix Lajkó. Lajkó has now moved on to a successful solo career, with a number of albums to

On the Opera House roof.

his credit. Perhaps the best is the wild, galloping *Lajkó Félix és Zenekara*. Dresch himself has yet to match his beautiful, lyrical early 90s CD *Zeng a Lélek*. László Hortobágyi creates electronic Indian fusion music in his Budapest studio. His album *Rosebuds in a Stoneyard* (also released as *Világfa*), with folk singer Irén Lovász, blends traditional Hungarian folk melodies with eastern rhythms to produce a haunting and original work.

OPERA

The Hungarian National Opera is in something of a cleft stick at the moment. Despite the encroachment of tourist busloads and block bookings by hotels for inflated prices, seats are still well on the good side of affordable. The quality of the opera itself, on the other hand, is inconsistent. Nevertheless, the sheer grandeur of the building makes a trip to the opera a must for all visitors to Budapest. Cultivate the *belle époque* attitude: the point of going to the opera is not for the opera itself but for the occasion. Reserve yourself a box, arrange for the ushers to bring you glasses of dry Tokaj Szamorodni in one of the intervals, stroll down to the buffet in the other, and slip out before the third act,

when the voluminous heroine breaks into a caterwaul prior to stabbing herself to the heart.

The opera building was designed by Miklós Ybl (*see p. 20*), and decorated inside with gorgeous allegorical frescoes by Bertalan Székely and Károly Lotz among others. Outside, the entrance is flanked by seated statues of Liszt and Ferenc Erkel, composer of Hungary's favourite national opera, *Bánk Bán*. Above these two stand the muses Erato, Thalia, Melpomene and Terpsichore, their names picked out in gilded Greek lettering. The Opera is said to have cost a million forints in gold to build, money which was entirely put up by the Emperor Franz Joseph, keen to demonstrate that he wasn't a Habsburg ogre - though he received little recognition for his generosity. To be fair, though, he in turn gave little recognition to the architect. "It is very beautiful. I like it very much," was all the effusion he could muster which, for what is arguably the loveliest opera house in Europe, is not saying much. The architect of the Vienna Opera, when faced with a similar lack of Imperial enthusiasm, had despairingly committed suicide.

The Opera's list of musical directors is distinguished: Gustav Mahler, Otto Klemperer and János Ferencsik have all been among them. Ferencsik

died in 1984, and since then the Opera has never regained its musical brilliance. The brilliance of the gold chandeliers and marble statues, however, remains, and a night here is simply fun. If you would like to see it in the daytime, more at leisure, guided tours in English start at 3pm and 4pm.

See Map References on p. 185 to locate the places mentioned in this section.

Tickets are available from the Liszt Academy from 10am to 1pm and 2pm to 8pm Mon-Fri, and 2pm to 8pm Sat-Sun.
The ticket office at the Opera House is open at the following times:

Mon: 11am-5pm;
Tue-Sun: 11am-6pm or 7pm, or until just before the performance starts for last-minute tickets.

Tickets to most concerts are also available from the Vigadó Ticket Centrum in the Vigadó office building at Pest V, Vörösmarty tér 1. Open Mon-Fri 9am-7pm and Sat-Sun 10am-3pm. If they have no tickets for the event you want, they will be able to suggest where to get them.

*Places marked with an asterisk require a full city map, available from bookshops.

PLACES TO GO

HEROES' SQUARE

This extravagant parade-ground was laid out for Hungary's "Millennium" celebrations of 1896, when the country celebrated 1,000 years since Árpád and his men streamed into the Carpathian basin to occupy the area for the Magyars. Actually, conventional history puts Árpád's arrival at about a year or two before 896 - but the story goes that the Millennium monuments were not ready in time, so Hungary officially and pragmatically pushed history back a bit. Heroes' Square is flanked by two Hellenistic buildings, the Palace of Art (Műcsarnok) and the Fine Arts Museum (*see p. 47*), while in the centre is a tall column topped by an image of the Archangel Gabriel. The reason for Gabriel's prominent position is because according to the story, he came down from

Leaders of the seven original Magyar tribes, together with other heroes from Hungarian history, line up in the pantheon of fame at Hősök tere.

heaven and suggested to Pope Sylvester that he send King Stephen a crown to seal his legitimacy. Today that crown is displayed in the Hungarian Parliament (*see pp. 142-3*). Behind Gabriel's column, in stately file, are the seven Magyar chieftains and other heroes of Hungarian history - carefully vetted by the Communists, who removed the statues of undesirable Habsburgs, replacing them with Hungarian freedom-fighters and Protestants - guaranteed to be anathema to old Catholic Austria. Today the square fills up with revellers on New Year's Eve, and with concerts and celebrations in June, commemorating the *Búcsú*, or final departure of Soviet soldiers, in 1990.

CITY PARK
(VÁROSLIGET)

Originally known as the City Woods, this area was once much more densely forested, and in mediaeval times was a royal hunting ground. The first documented story concerning the area is a sad one for Hungary. The wily Mongol leader Batu Khan (grandson of Genghis) staged a fake retreat in 1241, and

when the Hungarians arrived on the scene to make sure he was really going, his men ambushed them, trapped them in the boggy marsh that covered the area in those days, and shot them down with a hailstorm of arrows.

In the mid-18th century the area was given to the city, and planted with mulberry trees to feed silk worms. Pest was famously plagued by dust storms, and when the park was developed further, more trees were planted to try and contain the billowing clouds that were stirred up

Hairband seller on Heroes' Square.

by every passing carriage or puff of wind. In the savage winter of 1830, when the Palatine of Hungary, Archduke Joseph, ordered many of the trees to be cut down and used as firewood for the poor, several worthy burghers rose up in indignation, including István Széchenyi himself. Today the park is in rather scruffy condition, but contains several things that are worth a visit:

THE VÁROSLIGETI TÓ (CITY PARK LAKE)

In summer it is purely ornamental (though a bit grubby!), but in winter it turns into one of the most spectacular skating rinks anywhere. Lit up at night, with the turreted Vajdahunyad Castle as a backdrop, it is a wonderful sight. It is also a good place to learn to skate: there is nothing to hold on to, so once you are on the ice, there's nothing for it but to launch out. Skates can be hired at the rink, and mulled wine is on sale to give you extra courage. *Open Mon-Fri 9am-1pm and 4pm-8pm, Sat-Sun 10am-2pm and 4pm-8pm.*

VAJDAHUNYAD CASTLE

The castle itself is an architectural folly, constructed as a temporary gimmick for the 1896 "Millennium"

celebrations (see above) - but it proved so popular that it was rebuilt to last, and has been there ever since. The architect who designed it (Ignác Alpár) was given the brief to include sections representing every single architectural style to be found in Hungary. The part facing the lake is a copy of the Vajdahunyad Castle in what is now Hunedoara, Romania; hence the folly's name. It now hous-

Ice-skating on the rink in City Park, with the Vajdahunyad Castle as a backdrop.

es the Agricultural Museum, which is full of marvellous steam-powered leviathans for threshing and winnowing, and Stalinist-era posters of beaming peasants and muscular farm hands.

THE ZOO

This small zoo (at Állatkerti körút 6) is as humane and progressive as funding will allow. The best thing about it is its architecture: it boasts a couple of beautiful Art Nouveau enclosures: an Elephant House that looks like something out of the Arabian Nights, a turreted bird

house by Károly Kós (see p. 23), filled with free-flying birds, whizzing over your head, and a graceful parabolic palm house.

THE FUNFAIR (VIDÁMPARK)

Next door to the Zoo is the rundown City Circus and beside that is the Vidámpark. Almost the only truly beautiful thing in this woefully tatty jumble of collapsing rides is the lovely carousel, dated 1906, with its painted chariots, bugle-blowing angels and torch-bearing nymphs. There is also a wooden roller coaster,

The flamingo pond at the Budapest Zoo.

a very early example of the genre. In the twenties the playwright Ferenc Molnár set his work *Liliom* here, later reincarnated as the Hollywood musical *Carousel*.

Petőfi Csarnok (Fleamarket)

Revolutionary poet Sándor Petőfi would probably jump right out of his grave if he saw the cultural centre named after him in the centre of City Park: finding the entrance to the Petőfi Csarnok concert hall and cultural centre takes a degree in Communist-era ergonomics. However, it is redeemed by its fleamarket, held on Saturday and Sunday mornings, where for a token fee you can rifle through as much tat as your heart desires. Transylvanian shawls, tarnished silverware, nylon wigs, plastic beads and radio sets guaranteed never to work again are all on offer and, this being Hungary, food and drink are also readily available if you tire of bargaining.

Margaret Island

"The Margaret Isle is Budapest's cameo, a gem in itself, made yet more precious by cutting", wrote the novelist Mór Jókai. He was exaggerating a bit, though in early summer when the leaves are still fresh and the horse chestnuts are in flower, it is a pretty place to wander. Don't look at things too closely, though. Poor Margaret Island is in a rather run-down state, and crying out for city funding. In Jókai's day the island was owned by the Habsburg Archduke Joseph, who was responsible for building hotels and restaurants, as well as for turning its hot spring into a thermal bath. In its heyday that bath was one of the most beautiful in the city. Sadly it was badly damaged in the Second World War, and then again by flooding in the fifties. Now the spa is housed in a staggered-level seventies construction of staggering unloveliness.

In the early Middle Ages the island was known as Rabbit Island, and was stocked with game for royal hunting parties. At one time it boasted churches, nunneries, a monastery, the Archbishop of Esztergom's manse and a royal residence - until the Turks came and razed the whole lot to the ground, converting the island into a harem for a succession of priapic Pashas. Under cover of dusk, many a lusty young Hungarian lad would swim out to the island (this was in the days before bridges), to spy on the women. For most of the 19th century the island was a favourite strolling place for well-to-do families. The melancholy and much-beloved romantic poet János Arany came here every summer to write increasingly awful verse and take the medicinal waters for his gall stones. Since 1908 the island has been a public park, boasting swimming pools, stalls selling snacks, ornamental gardens, lawns and fountains, and benches to sit on and soak up some sun and fresher air.

The best single sight are the ruins of the Dominican convent, on the east of the island (the right hand side if you approach from Margaret Bridge) about halfway up. It was here that Margaret, the island's namesake, lived out her brief life - a red marble slab marks the spot where her tomb lay (it and her remains were smuggled to Bratislava after the Ottoman invasion) and a little shrine dedicated to her, filled with plastic

flowers and grateful plaques, testifies to her enduring popularity. The story goes that Margaret's father, King Béla IV, whose reign was plagued by the threat of Mongol invasion, pledged that if he managed to keep the marauders at bay, he would dedicate his child to God. He won his bet, and Margaret entered the nunnery in 1252 at the age of 9. Convent life took its psychological toll, turning her into a fierce ascetic and mortifier of the flesh. But "her rough woollen garments were not sufficient concealment for her extraordinary charms", we are told: King Ottokar of Bohemia offered to marry her in 1262. Margaret replied that she had taken the veil that very same year and had

Horse chestnut trees in flower among the ruins on Margaret Island.

no intention of retracting her vows. She went back to her punishing routine of scrubbing the nunnery corridors and tending the victims of diseases so nauseating that other nuns had been frightened away. She refused to wash above her ankles, and dressed herself in rough hair shirts which she secured at the waist with hedgehog skins. As a result of these unhygienic practices, the stench of her sanctity was legendary and the decline in her health rapid. She died at the age of 29, a martyr to her country's cause. Shortly before her death she gave the keys of her trunk to the Mother Superior. Crowds gathered to witness the trunk's opening, convinced that it contained precious treasure. All they found were two rough-woven shifts, an iron belt studded with pointed nails, a leather whip, and two pairs of stockings lined with iron spikes. Margaret was finally canonised in 1943. Now someone has written an opera about her. They say that if you stand at a certain point on the island on the day of her death (February 15th), a marvellous light suffuses the air, coupled with a delicious perfume and the sound of high-pitched singing, and flickering blue flames guide you to buried treasure. This has never been proven, though the island did at one time fall prey to a rash of hopeful excavators.

GELLÉRT HILL

The Citadel on top of Gellért Hill is the best place for a view of the city. The Habsburgs were well aware of this, which is why they built the fortress here after the suppression of the 1848 revolution. Gun shafts point at the Danube and down into Pest, as well as to the Buda Hills behind. But it was more for show than anything else; they wanted to remind a rebellious population who was in charge - and it worked: the Hungarians called it the Budapest Bastille, and universally loathed it. It was finally handed over to the City Council in 1897, but somehow never got knocked down.

A similar story is attached to the Liberation Monument in front of it. This enormous female statue was designed originally to carry a propeller blade, to commemorate the death in an air crash of the son of Admiral Horthy, Hungary's inter-war Regent. The statue did not go up until 1947, however, by which time historical events had overtaken Horthy. The propellor blade was substituted for a palm frond, stalwart Soviet soldiers were added around the base, and the whole sculpture was dubbed the Liberation Monument, the "liberation" in question being that of Budapest by the Red Army. Though the statue has been reprieved and not carted off to the out-of-town Statue Park (*see pp. 48-9*) with almost all the city's other Soviet monuments, the names of the Soviet soldiers who died fighting the Nazis have all been picked off - but nevertheless it remains, like the Citadel, despite being a reminder of a hated regime.

Gellért Hill has a tarnished reputation in other ways, too. According to folk tradition, it was the spot where witches from all over the country used to convene, summoned by the devil in the form of a raven or black crow. It is also the site of the murder of Bishop Gellért, the Venetian primate who had helped King Stephen to convert his people to Christianity, and who acted as tutor to Stephen's sickly son Imre. Gellért was brutally clubbed to death by jealous pagan chieftains, who then rolled his body into the river below. Legend says that it took seven years to wash the stones clean of his blood. His statue now presides over the hillside overlooking Elisabeth Bridge, with an ornamental waterfall trickling downwards from it.

On an outcrop opposite the entrance to the Gellért Baths is a large natural cave, once inhabited by a charitable hermit called Iván, who used to heal the sick with the aid of curative waters that bubbled up from a spring near the cave entrance. In the mid-1920s the cave was turned into a chapel, modelled on the one at Lourdes. The chapel was run by the Paulines, the only monastic order of Hungarian origin, who take their name from Paul, a saint from 3rd-century Egypt, who fled into the desert to escape persecution. According to the legend, Paul lived a life of total solitude, with only a raven for company, who brought him food - half a slice of bread a day. The Communists seized the chapel in the 1950s, dissolved the order, executed the Father Superior, and walled the chapel up. When the Church got it back in 1989, they preserved a great lump of reinforced concrete from this wall, which you can see at the entrance to the cave. Inside, the cave is composed of a string of natural hollows, each containing a small chapel. They are not particularly beautiful, but the whole complex is made interesting and moving by its history. In the central chapel there is a little statue of St Paul, with his raven sitting on his shoulder. The old raven-devil of mediaeval magic tradition seems to have come home to roost in a more benign guise.

KEREPESI CEMETERY
(Pest VIII, Fiumei út 16)

There is nothing remotely gloomy about this beautiful place; its tranquillity and its greenery make it arguably the best "park" in the city. And whether you want to seek out the graves of the famous or infamous, or simply wander among the unknown dead, the architecture of the mausoleums and headstones makes it well worth the effort to get there. The best way is to take the red metro

Carousel in the old Vidámpark funfair (see p. 62 above).

line to Keleti Pályaudvar, from where it is a few minutes walk up Fiumei út. (The street sign is still the old one, Mező Imre út, and though the name has been crossed out in angry red, the sign has not been replaced. You will meet Imre Mező again in a few minutes).

Once inside the main gates, purchase a map from the information window on your left. The flower shop opposite has newer maps, but they are much less helpful than the detailed 1990 version. You can gauge political affiliations and the mood of the nation by the flowers deposited on the graves here. The contrasting gardens of remembrance for 1956 have a tale to tell: the urns of those who fought for the Soviets can be found in the plot marked by a bold 15 on the map. "Eternal gratitude and honour to the heroes who fell in the struggle against the counter-revolution" reads the legend on the central sarcophagus. Despite this grandiloquence, the place has a - literally - dead feel to it, quite at odds with the burgeoning trees and flowers you will find at plot number 14, a living garden in memory of those who fought against Red Russia. Just in front of this is a newish-looking plot which every year has more tenants. These are returnees, exiles who left Hungary during troubled times, but who have returned to rest in its soil. The Pantheon to the Workers' Movement is another must (No. 11). Enormous and once gleaming white, it is now dusty and dishevelled and gone out of fashion like a closed-down clubhouse. "They lived for the People and for Communism" blares the bold black lettering. No one now seems to care. Certainly not the people. Some of the graves are still tend-

ed - most are forgotten and overgrown. An air of dereliction hangs over the whole place, and grass and weeds are slowly breaking up the paving stones. One of the graves contains Imre Mező himself, the man who briefly gave his name to Fiumei út. Though he died in 1956, of wounds sustained in the "counter revolution", he seems not quite forgotten - perhaps because his wife Mariska only joined him in 1995.

Very near here is the red marble grave of Hungary's last Communist premier, János Kádár (d. 1989). He competes in floral tributes with József Antall, first Prime Minister of a democratic Hungary (d. 1993), who lies in splendid isolation in the middle of plot number 28. Antall generally wins the contest, but Kádár is by no means unremembered or unbeloved.

The most pompous monuments of all are those to Deák, Batthyány and Kossuth (see p. 17). Kossuth's is the best: a triumph of majesty and vainglory in limestone and bronze, guarded by two crouching pumas. Nearby is a triangle-shaped plot lined with the black marble graves of Communist stalwarts and their wives.

Round the back of the Kerepesi, on Salgótarjáni utca, is the entrance to the Jewish Cemetery, which served wealthy families before the Second World War. Industrialists like Weiss and Goldberger are to be found here, in wonderful tombs designed by Béla Lajta (see p. 22), who also designed the entranceway. The lack of relatives left to care for the graves today means that the cemetery is sadly overgrown and tangled.

Kerepesi is open daily 7am to 5.30pm (8pm in summer). The Jewish cemetery is open Sun-Fri 8am-4pm.

See Map References on p. 185 to locate these places to go.

PHOTOGRAPHY

During the first half of the century Hungary produced some of the world's finest photographers. They include:

ANDRÉ KERTÉSZ
(1894-1985) - As a young man he took part in and photographed World War I. He was invalided out and sent to a sanatorium where there was an exercise pool, and it was then that he began work on his great series of swimmers. He was primarily interested in the way the water distorted the body, and later, in his studio in Paris, where he settled until the Second World War, he even set up a distorting mirror through which he would photograph his models and subjects. Throughout his long life he continued to be fascinated by the idea that there is a dissonance to be found in even the most harmonious subjects.

LÁSZLÓ MOHOLY-NAGY
(1895-1946) - One of the great avant-garde artists of his day, Moholy-Nagy also invented the photogram, an image produced by placing objects on light-sensitive paper and exposing them to various degrees of light. He left Hungary after the 1919 Commune was declared, and went to work in Berlin, becoming a colleague of the Bauhaus teacher W. Gropius. Fleeing Hitler's Germany, he eventually settled in Chicago, where he set up the New Bauhaus.

GEORGES BRASSAÏ
(1899-1984) - Famed for his fabulous 1930s Paris by Night series, Brassaï also took portrait photos of Picasso, Matisse and the beau monde of the time. His iconic shots of streetlife and spontaneous roving photos of lovers in parks influenced generations of young photographers

LUCIEN HERVÉ
(1910 -) - Hailed by Le Corbusier as a photographer with the soul of an architect, Hervé is most famous for his beautifully-realised shots of buildings and architectural details. These range from ruined Indian palaces to barely-finished modern designs. Hervé, like Kertész, left Hungary for Paris in the twenties, and met and photographed many of the great artists and thinkers who flocked there in the early 20th century.

ROBERT CAPA
(1913-1954) - Perhaps one of the founders of documentary photography, Capa spent the twenties roaming Europe and earned his name for his depictions of the Spanish Civil War. He then went on to work as a US army photographer during World War II, taking some extraordinary pictures of the liberation of Paris. In 1947 he set up the Magnum Photographic Agency with Henri Cartier-Bresson, only to be killed on assignment in Vietnam in 1954 when he stepped on a landmine.

The Mai Manó House of Hungarian Photography at Nagymező utca 20 has collections of these photographers' works.

RELIGIOUS MONUMENTS

Most of the smaller churches in Budapest keep their doors locked unless there is a service on.
In others the main doors are open, but you can get up to the inner door and no further. Below
are places that you can (usually) visit at leisure.

ST STEPHEN'S
BASILICA
Pest V, Szent István tér

This church had an incredibly long gestation period: construction took over fifty years, between 1851 and 1906, and its slowness became such a local joke that the expression "when the Basilica is fin-ished" became a sort of Hungarian equivalent of "pigs might fly". It is the work of three architects, which perhaps explains why the building somehow fails to come across as a convincing whole. József Hild started the project, and is responsible for the neo-Classical east and west facades. After his death, Miklós Ybl (see pp. 20-21) took over, and put up

The main west door of St Stephen's Basilica.

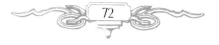
the neo-Renaissance main entrance and the façade flanking Bajcsy-Zsilinszky út. But when he also died, the Basilica still wasn't finished, and another man was brought in to complete the job. Nothing went smoothly for this church. In the 1860s, the first dome collapsed and had to be completely remodelled. When the inaugural mass at last took place, in 1906, Emperor Franz Joseph was seen to look nervously up at the ceiling to make sure it wasn't caving in.

The interior of the Basilica was decorated by notable artists of the day, who contributed frescoes, and statues whose subjects aim to link Hungarian history to Christianity - not always a straightforward task. St. Stephen, to whom the Basilica is dedicated, originally went under the pagan name Vajk, but became a Christian and set about using Christianity ruthlessly, to unite the warring tribes that fought for control of the Hungarian lands. He succeeded, more or less, and was the first crowned Christian monarch of a united Hungary. His statue stands on the high altar, and his embalmed right hand is kept here too, revered as a cult relic. You can see it displayed in its jewelled casket, in a separate chapel to the left of the altar.

In the summer months you can climb to the top of the dome, and enjoy a splendid city panorama. Coming back down to earth again, it is odd to realise that the grand carved tympanum announcing "the way, the truth and the life" contains a public toilet.

MÁTYÁS CHURCH
Buda I, Szentháromság tér

Notoriously difficult to photograph, though a prime tourist attraction, this church must be responsible for more postcards than any other monument in Budapest. Large and imposing, the Mátyás Church is somehow not very beautiful - at least not in its present incarnation. In its 750-year history it has had several. It was founded in 1255, and dedicated to the Blessed Virgin, by King Béla IV, after he moved his court up to Castle Hill from Óbuda. It gets its popular name from an escutcheon bearing the coat of arms of King Mátyás Corvinus (reigned 1458-1490), which you can see about halfway up the outside of the south tower. The lower section of this tower is the original 13th-century Gothic. Mátyás married twice, both times in this church. His first wife was the twelve-year-old daughter of Podjebrad of Bohemia, who died almost immediately because, as one writer darkly expressed it, "her tender body was not strong enough to

withstand the rigours of cohabitation". His second wife Beatrice, daughter of the King of Naples, was made of much robuster stuff. She encouraged him to patronise the arts, and he left off his youthful Turk-bashing to embellish his palaces in incredible style and generally turn himself into a true Renaissance monarch. When the Turks finally captured Buda in 1541, they transformed the church into a mosque, and held a celebration here to mark their victory. Jesuit zeal removed any trace of Ottomanisation after the Christians won Buda back a century and a half later, though the

church building in those days was modest and rather squat. After the 1867 Compromise Agreement between Hungary and Austria (*see p. 13*), Emperor Franz Joseph was crowned here. Services in those days were held in German. The Hungarian-speaking minority on Castle Hill was catered for by the Church of Mary Magdalene on Országház utca (now a ruin). In preparation for Hungary's "Millennium" celebrations in 1896, the church was completely remodelled, though what remained of the original 13th-century stonework was incorporated into the new design.

Detail of Gothic stonework on the Mátyás Church.

The result is a ponderous 19th-century fantasy of what the mediaeval original might have looked like, concocted by the architect Frigyes Schulek, who is also responsible for the stage-set Fishermen's Bastion (*see p. 82*). The interior of the Mátyás Church, with its exuberantly painted columns using geometric designs, supposedly Turkish, and floral patterns inspired by Hungarian folk

motifs, is certainly striking, but it is difficult to say that it inspires awe. Though the fresco artists, Károly Lotz and Bertalan Székely, were some of Hungary's finest of the period, the late 19th century was a profoundly secular age, quite at odds with the Gothic spirit. The resulting church is impressive but somehow spiritually unsatisfying.

THE UNIVERSITY CHURCH
Pest V, Egyetem tér

This church, on Egyetem tér (University Square) in central Pest, is one of the prettiest in town. It is also a church whose Baroque style mercifully hasn't been tampered with. The original building dates from 1722-42, and though it was renovated twice since, and had to be restored following damage in World War II, the restoration was sensitively and faithfully carried out. The church was originally a Pauline foundation, the Paulines being the only monastic order of Hungarian origin. Make sure you notice the beautifully carved main door, showing a pelican plucking her breast to feed her chicks (symbol of Christ's sacrifice) and a phoenix rising from the ashes

Interior of the University Church.

Interior of the Great Synagogue on Dohány utca, the largest synagogue in Europe.

(symbol of the Resurrection). These carvings were the work of a Pauline monk called Brother Felix, also responsible for the beautiful pulpit and choir stall doors. The church was completed in 1742, but the Paulines lost it less than half a century later, when the Emperor Joseph II dissolved their order and gave their church to the University.

SYNAGOGUES & JEWISH MONUMENTS

The Dohány utca Synagogue is situated at an angle to Múzeum körút, between Deák tér and Astoria. If you duck into some of the courtyards on the further side of Múzeum körút, you will see traces of the old Pest city walls. It is no coincidence that the

Gül Baba's tomb on the Hill of Roses (Rózsadomb) in Buda.

synagogue sits just outside the old city limits, for Jews were forbidden to live in the city - and so, in the 18th century, they established a Jewish quarter for themselves just outside the walls, and built their main synagogue there, staring defiantly back at the Roman Catholic town. This arresting building, completed in 1862, was built by a Viennese architect in a romantic fusion of pseudo-Moorish and pseudo-Byzantine. It is the second largest synagogue in the world, with seating capacity for almost 3,000: men downstairs, and women in the first-floor gallery. In the courtyard behind the main building is a moving memorial by the sculptor Imre Varga. It takes the form of a metal weeping wil-

low tree, planted on the site of the mass graves of victims of the Holocaust. Each leaf bears the name of one of the dead. In 1944 an enclosed ghetto was created, the gates to which were just alongside the synagogue, in Wesselényi utca. A small plaque now commemorates this fact. There is also a Jewish museum in one wing of the synagogue with ancient Jewish ritual objects as well as a harrowing exhibition on the Holocaust in Hungary. A plaque on the main façade commemorates Theodore Herzl, father of Zionism, who was born here in 1860 (see pp. 151-2).

Close by the main synagogue are two others, an old conservative one in Rumbach Sebestyén utca (see p. 133), which is no longer in use, and

an orthodox one in Kazinczy utca (*see p. 155*). A restoration programme began on the first, but sadly the money ran out and it has come to a standstill. Work is still underway on the Kazinczy utca one. *Tours of Jewish Budapest can be booked from Chosen Tours, T: 355-2202 (not Saturdays).*

GÜL BABA'S TOMB
Buda II, Mecset utca 14

Though not strictly a place of worship, Muslims have traditionally regarded this place as holy. Gül Baba was a Dervish who came to Buda with the Ottoman invaders in 1541. He then died of overexcitement at the thanksgiving ceremony held in the Mátyás Church-turned-mosque, and was buried in the place where his tomb now stands. Just outside the railed-off precinct is a statue of him - at least, of an artist's impression of what he was like. Legend remembers him as a great horticulturalist, responsible for introducing cultivated roses into Hungary (his name, in fact, roughly translates as "Rose Daddy"). His tomb and the ornamental garden around it were restored in 1997, with money given by the Turkish government. Once a rather mystic place, where Muslims would always devoutly remove their shoes, it is now a little sterile. Time should cure that, however. The tomb is a small octagonal, domed building, built between 1543 and 1548. It was turned into a Christian chapel by the Jesuits in 1690, but this is the only blip in a continuous Muslim tradition. Inside, the walls have been hung with modern ceramic dishes inscribed with Koranic verses, and Gül Baba's sarcophagus lies draped in a cloth embroidered with gold. The view from the garden's colonnaded parapet is good: the tiled rooftops of lower Buda, Margaret Bridge, and a shining sliver of the Danube. And there are roses planted in the garden.

See Map References on p. 185 to locate these buildings.

PART III

GUIDED WALKS

These walks, blending history, architecture, culture and local tradition, are designed to take a maximum of 1 hour each.
By visiting museums or coffee houses along the way, you can spin them out into half a morning or afternoon. Refreshments are always included en route. Museums or other major sights included in the itinerary are cross-referenced to the pages in Part II of the book, where they are dealt with in detail.

Key streets and sights are marked in bold throughout.

CASTLE HILL

The most scenic district of Buda, where solidly prosperous Baroque town houses mingle with vestiges of mediaeval splendour and the constant reminders of battles lost and won. In its time Castle Hill has been fought over by Ottomans and Christians, Habsburgs and Hungarians, Soviets and Nazis.

took Buda in 1541 without a shot being fired. The area remained in Ottoman hands for a hundred and fifty years, until a successful but destructive siege in 1686, led by the Habsburg armies, claimed the palace for the Holy Roman (Austrian) Emperor. Or rather, they claimed

This walk starts in Szentháromság tér, Holy Trinity Square, in the **Ruszwurm café**, the oldest café in the city (founded in 1827). It is tiny and elegant, non-smoking, and renowned for its pastries (*see p. 35*). You are in the heart of Castle Hill, a limestone outcrop rising steeply on the western bank of the Danube, and chosen as the site for the Royal Palace in the 13th century, after a massive Mongol invasion had swept across the country, killing subjects and destroying the kingdom. King Béla IV decided to move his castle from Óbuda, north of the present site, downriver to this higher, safer location. For three centuries after that, Hungarian monarchs occupied Castle Hill, until Sultan Suleiman

Plague monument outside the Mátyás Church celebrating Buda's deliverance from the dreaded black death in 1713.

what was left of it. During the reign of King Mátyás (1458-1490) the palace was completely rebuilt in the Renaissance style, and contemporary accounts marvel at its splendour, claiming that even in the whole of Italy there was no finer building. In 1663 the Turkish chronicler Evlia Celebi wrote that as soon as he saw the palace, he dropped to his knees and touched his forehead to the ground, giving thanks to Allah for allowing him to see Buda. But the siege of 1686 left it hopelessly ruined, along with most of the rest of the city. Only a few hundred people were left alive out of a population of thousands. The city was rebuilt in the Baroque style, and it prospered once again, but somehow its splendour had gone. The royal court no longer sat here, and the aristocracy drifted away. Buda became home to a mainly German-speaking community of shopkeepers, merchants and artisans.

Come out of the Ruszwurm now and turn left. In front of you will see the **Mátyás Church** (*see p. 72*) and **Fishermen's Bastion** (so-named, according to one tradition, because it stands on the site of the mediaeval fish market). "Kitsch but beautiful" was the thirties writer Antal Szerb's verdict on the Fishermen's Bastion. Its great advantage, whatever you think of it, is that

from the top of it you get one of the greatest views the city has to offer. Nestling in its embrace is an equestrian **statue of King Stephen** (*see p. 11*). Go towards the bastion now, and cross **Szentháromság tér**, which is marked by a votive monument erected in 1713 after a series of plagues had swept through the city. Veer left towards the Hilton Hotel, which preys on two fine old buildings. It was cobbled together by Béla Pintér in 1976 out of the remains of a 13th century Dominican monastery (the lower part of the tower of which still stands) and a former Jesuit College built in the Zopf style. On the old monastery tower you will see a relief (allegedly a faithful portrait) of King Mátyás, hailed as Hungary's greatest ruler. A true renaissance prince, he was at once bibliophile and hunter, scholar and sovereign. His legend lives on, and children are still told of how he roamed the country in disguise, intervening in village arguments and rows between neighbours, using his wit and patience to pacify his quarrelsome subjects. It was during his reign that the following Italian saying was coined: "Europe has three pearls of cities: Venice on the Water, Buda on the Hill and Florence on the Plain". Mátyás was only 47 when he died, and his death is shrouded in mystery.

Some say he died at the hands of his duplicitous queen Beatrice, others that a palace uprising struck him down in his prime. But these are probably just more examples of the thousands of fables that surround him. Whatever the case, he died leaving Hungary a dominant force in Europe, with control over Bohemia, Silesia, Moravia and even lower Austria.

Opposite the Mátyás relief is a statue of Pope Innocent XI, the man on whose initiative a pan-Christian army joined forces against the Turk in 1686. This square is said to be the place where the last Pasha of Buda, Abdurrahman, fell. Behind Pope Innocent is the old Vörös Sün (Red Hedgehog) inn, with a red plaster hedgehog above its main entrance.

The Erdődy Palace, where Beethoven once stayed, now the Music History Museum.

This was the first inn in Buda, later home to the architect Matthias Nepauer, whom you will meet later.

Take the road to the right of the inn now. This is **Táncsics Mihály utca**. Look at No. 6 and you will see how mediaeval remains were incorporated into the new Baroque town. Each house had its own well, wine cellar and grain store beneath it. No. 5 opposite used to be the ice-chamber of the Turkish janissaries. At No. 9, formerly the city gaol, you will see the likenesses of Lajos Kossuth and Mihály Táncsics, who were imprisoned here in the 1840s for their activities in the cause of Hungarian independence from Austria. Táncsics, famous for his excoriating delivery and radical passion, was not much liked by the authorities on account of such declarations as: "Patriots, my worker brothers! Listen well to my words: there are no more lords and peasants, there are no serfs, people will not be beaten any more; we are all equal citizens and brothers". Originally a barracks, this building, with its two-metre-thick walls, became a prison for so-called "status prisoners" in the period leading up to the 1848 revolution. Another famous figure who stayed in this street - although presumably not in such straitened circumstances - was Beethoven who, as a guest of the

Erdődy family, visited the **Erdődy Palace**, next door at No. 7. This fine mid-18th century building was built by Nepauer, the architect who lived in the old inn on the corner. The male heads on the pilasters supporting the first floor balcony are said to be self-portraits. The palace now houses the Music History Museum, where you will find the Bartók archives as well as collections of ancient instruments. In the summer,

concerts are held in the courtyard, and there is a lovely garden at the back with views over the river into Pest.

Walk on up the street now, passing No. 17, formerly home to Albert Apponyi, a liberal politician who was thrown out of Parliament in 1912 when he and his supporters rioted against the Prime Minister. A great patriot, he was forever campaigning to make the Austro-Hungarian Empire more visibly Hungarian rather than simply Austrian. When these campaigns extended to Magyarising non-Hungarian ethnic minorities within Hungary, however, he met resistance and resentment. His son was taken from this house to Mauthausen (a concentration camp close to Dachau) by the Nazis. The modern green building at No. 20 is a brave experiment. When the Red Army finally drove the Nazis from Buda in 1945, only four houses were left in a habitable condition. Most were simply rebuilt exactly as they had been before, but one or two attempts at something new were made - some more successful than others. No. 26, a little further on, contains the **Sephardic Prayer House**, established in the mid 16th century by the Sephardic Jews, who came in the wake of the Ottoman army. This

street was then known as Jew Street, and the small Sephardic community lived and traded here for one and half centuries, along with the Ashkenazi community which was already present. This tiny prayer house (open May-October 10am-5pm, except Mon) is all that remains of Jewish life in the Castle District. When on September 2nd 1686 the armies of the Holy Roman Emperor took back the Buda Castle, four and a half centuries of Jewish life in Buda were wiped out. Jewish elders issued rat poison to their community on the eve of the battle, so terrified were they of the Christian onslaught. Many fought alongside the Ottomans, who had allowed them to trade freely and had not restricted them to usury as many previous reigns had done. A contemporary general, Johann Dietz, writes that the women were rounded up and taken to Berlin where they were married off to the German nobility. Jews were not allowed to settle in the Castle District again until nearly two centuries later, when the Compromise of 1867 (*see p. 13*) was disposed to be lenient towards them.

Leaving the prayer house, go straight ahead until you come out into a wide square. This is **Bécsi kapu tér**, (Vienna Gate Square) dominated by the lugubrious neo-

Gothic National Archives, built in 1913 by the same man who built the Central Market Hall in Pest (*see pp. 137 & 138*) - this is not nearly such a successful project. In fact the building is so gloomy that when the Soviet tanks rolled in in 1956 to suppress the anti-Stalinist revolution, they mistook the place for a barracks and bombarded it. The tiles on the roof represent medals slung from Hungarian tricolor ribbon, and the owls guarding the entranceway testify to the building's serious intent. Otherwise this is a delightful square of Baroque buildings. In the 18th century Nos. 5 and 6 were home to a family of blacksmiths - possibly responsible for all the wrought ironwork in front of so many groundfloor windows in this district. The two houses have a common roof because, as tradition says, the son of one house married the daughter of the other, and their parents decided to "unite the two families under a single roof".

Climb up to the top of the Vienna Gate now to admire the view on your left towards Moszkva tér and the poplar-covered Rózsadomb (Rose Hill), Buda's most exclusive residential area. It looks a lot better from a distance, as faithful cadres, scrambling for a good address in the sixties and seventies, coated it with con-

crete blocks and much of its original charm has been lost. Leave the gate now, going down to your left and along a path that leads behind the Archives. Follow the line of the old fortifications until you come to a turban-topped stone stele. This is the **tomb of Abdurrahman Pasha**, who died in 1686, "on the afternoon of the second day of the last month of summer" (September). "A valiant foe," reads the inscription, "peace be with him".

Carry on up the walkway past the ancient guns and cannons, at the end turn left round the corner and you come out in front of an imposing white-painted building, the **Military History Museum**. The cannonballs embedded in its outer wall are said to date from the 1849 battle in which the Hungarian rebel forces attempted to capture Buda from its Habsburg liegelords. It was a difficult battle to win, especially in Buda, where the ethnic German majority was not particularly supportive of the Magyar cause. When you reach the cannons of the Military History Museum, turn left into Kapisztrán tér. In doing this you are doing exactly what the Christian armies did in 1686, for it was here that they at last breached the walls and streamed into the city, despite the cannons that had been set up by the Turks in the **church tower of St Mary Magdalene**, which you will see ahead of you to the right. This church was badly bombed in World War II, and its 15th-century tower is more or less all that remains. Originally it was the church used by the Hungarian-speaking minority - German speakers heard mass in the Mátyás Church. During much of the Ottoman occupation all churches except this one were used as mosques, and the Christian communities in Buda all came to pray here, regardless of denomination. While the Counter Reformation raged in the rest of Europe, with the Inquisition sending thousands to the stake, religious tolerance was an important feature of the reign of the terrible Turks - at least at first. Eventually wearying of repeated Christian attempts to win back the city, the pashas converted this church into a mosque as well.

Go down **Úri utca** now. No. 58 is the former Royal Treasury, and even its drainpipes have crowns on them. Today it houses the district's registry office, and the façade, with its extraordinary array of symbols, dates from 1904. The back of the building is particularly fine, with a great Sun window radiating out on the upper floor and below it an ornate wrought iron balcony, the whole thing resplendent in Maria Theresa yellow, a colour which you can still find on palaces and public buildings all over the former Habsburg empire, from Romania to the Rhine. It is built in the Zopf style, which was favoured by Maria Theresa (1717-1780) and her son

Tomb of Abdurrahman, last Pasha of Buda, who fell in battle in 1686.

Joseph II (1741-90). Although inspired by the Louis XIV style, it was more restrained and less decorative than its French counterpart. The style takes its name from the German word for a plait (*Zopf*), a reference to the braided wigs which were popular during the period, and thus to the plait-like swags which are a key feature of Zopf decoration. Nos. 52 and 60 boast plaques commemorating the vindictiveness of two regimes. From No. 60 Count Antal Szigray was dragged away to Mauthausen by the Nazis. Count Zsigmond Széchenyi was evicted from No. 52 by the State Security Authority (ÁVH) in 1951, at a time when the Communists were sending the "class enemy" off to do forced labour and using their homes to house their apparatchiks.

Go on now until you reach the **Café Miró** on your left. If you feel surfeited on the past, this place, with its Surrealist wrought iron furniture, solarium-bronzed waitresses and selection of brandies, is guaranteed to return you to the modern world.

WALK TWO

KRISZTINAVÁROS

Leafy late 19th-century and early 20th-century residential streets give onto the bustling main artery of Christina Town and the historic Vérmező, now a leafy public park, but once the scene of mediaeval jousts and thwarted anti-monarchy plots.

This walk begins in the Café Miró on Castle Hill. Coming out of the café, leave the spire of the Mátyás Church behind you and turn immediately right into **Tóth Árpád sétány**. This pleasant leafy stretch was opened to the public in the 1810s, and became known as the Buda Promenade. Quartets played here every Sunday as respectable townsfolk strolled, and young actresses came looking for beaux. Today you will encounter rollerbladers, old ladies walking poodles, toddlers on tricycles, and young lovers skulking in the shadows. On a sunny day it is one of the pleasantest places to walk on the whole of Castle Hill, a far cry from how it was immediately after the Christian defeat of the Sultans in 1686, when the area around the castle became a restricted zone. Until the late 18th century, anything that came within rifle-range of the castle walls remained under military control.

Go down the covered steps ahead of you. You are leaving the Castle District now and coming into Krisztinaváros. A little to your right you will see the massive bulk of one of the Castle Hill's fortifying bastions. The bastions all along this defence wall were added to the mediaeval fortification by the Ottomans. Though they may look stout, they did little to help the Hungarians in their bid to liberate themselves from Habsburg rule in 1848 (*see p. 13*). This revolution, which had originally set out as a movement to abolish serfdom, got caught up in the tangle of its own nationalism, alienating the other large ethnic groups who lived in the old Kingdom of Hungary. The fiery romanticism of figures like Sándor Petőfi, who initiated the rebellion with a poem and died on the battlefield not long afterwards, at the age of twenty-six, had little appeal for the large Serb and Romanian minorities, who in turn revolted against the Magyars. In the end however, it was the Russians who put a stop to the proceedings. Franz Joseph appealed to Czar Nicholas to help him restore control; the Czar did not need much persuading, and the Russian army

marched in. A slight sense of *déjà vu* pervades all Hungarian history.

At the bottom of the steps, cross over the street to the bust of Károly P. Szathmáry (1830-1891). A writer, he fought at the tender age of 18 in the 1848 wars, and went on to become an MP in 1869 following the Compromise (*see p. 13*). It is the extraordinary truth that many who had been imprisoned or sentenced to death in absentia in 1849 - after the revolution was suppressed - later became statesmen in the Dual Monarchy. Count Gyula Andrássy, who had fled execution, actually stood next to Franz Joseph eighteen years later, in 1867, so that he, along with the Archbishop of Esztergom, could place the Hungarian crown on the Emperor's head. The quote on Szathmáry's bust reads: "Fool is he who gazes at the setting sun; there night approaches. I watch the rising sun alone, waiting for the break of the Hungarian dawn". The Hungarian dawn did break, but not quite in the way he had envisaged it: Hungary became a partner in the dual Austro-Hungarian Monarchy, Budapest became a united city, capital of Hungary, and Hungary enjoyed an extraordinary boom until the end of the century. P. Szathmáry's bust originally stood at the bottom of the steps facing east, until some bright spark pointed out that he was facing the sunset, at which point he was swiftly moved up here. The essayist Sándor Márai (1900-1989), who lived in this area, described Krisztinaváros as "leafy, slow-moving, full of middle-class retirees whose reserved good manners and insistence on good form exceed even English standards. Probably no one of my generation has heard of Károly P. Szathmáry, but in Krisztinaváros he is still in fashion".

Turn right now along **Lovas út**, once an area of farmland. It was only in 1769 that Maria Christina, Maria Theresa's daughter, gave permission to build here, and the burghers of Buda were so delighted at her altruism that this part of town was christened Krisztinaváros (Christina Town) in her honour. One or two villas sprang up, built by court officials who presided over the Emperor Joseph II's Regent's Council (the court proper sat at Bratislava), but even so the sleepy atmosphere prevailed, and still seems to prevail today. It is hard to imagine a thousand ladders being scaled and troops in scarlet and plumes stamping through the vines and meadows that covered these slopes. It wasn't until after the unification of Pest and Buda in 1873 that the Castle District

really began to hum with life again, and government ministries, with their attendant civil servants and their families, moved into the Krisztinaváros area. You can peer into some of the gardens and admire the wrought iron and adoring putti on the façade of No. 16 or the relief of St. George and the Dragon on the house at No. 6/B, further along, opposite another bulky bastion,

which overlooks a garden of fig trees. Next door there is nothing but a tangle of tumbleweed. A villa belonging to the celebrated thirties actress Gizi Bajor once stood here, but a direct hit flattened it during the Second World War. Bajor survived the war, only to be killed in the fifties by her husband, a Professor of Medicine. Without her knowledge he, in the belief that his beloved wife had a brain tumour, injected first her and then himself with a lethal dose of poison. A subsequent autopsy found no growth of any kind, and this post-war, middle-aged Romeo and Juliet have been a source of speculation ever since.

Go down steps of Bugát utca now, and into **Logodi utca**, a street with powerful literary associations. At the beginning of the century and between the wars, many writers wrote about and lived in this street, and thus it has gone down in the Hungarian imagination as a street of poets. Gyula Krúdy (1878-1933), who wrote incessantly and obsessively about Budapest, describes supple actresses being serenaded by their admirers as they sat in their boudoirs, while Sándor Márai declared that he felt he was entering

Tóth Árpád sétány, former military exercise ground turned pedestrian promenade.

a foreign land as soon as he crossed the river into Pest, and could only maintain his equilibrium if he stayed on the western bank of the river. Much has changed since they walked here; the last fifty years have wreaked havoc on this quiet lane and the travails of the 20th century are palpable on its pock-marked façades. Many are strafed with bullet holes, probably German fire intended to repel the Soviet army as it stormed the Castle in the final offensive in the spring of 1945. As the Soviet cordon tightened and the fighting took a desperate turn, many of these houses suffered irreparable damage, hence the amount of new building. When the Red Army eventually emerged victorious, it was left presiding over a mound of charred ruins. Many of the houses are still in a state of sorry disrepair. Note the building on the left-hand corner of the steps you have just come down. All you can see is exposed brickwork, the decorative plaster stucco having almost entirely fallen away.

Cross the street now and continue on down the Bugát steps. Immediately to your left a few blocks of stone stand out of the ground like stumpy teeth in an ancient jawbone.

Old apartment block on Logodi utca. Note how it has lost all its stucco work.

These are the ruins of ancient **church of Logod**, Logod being the small hamlet that gave its name to the street you have just left. Millions of years ago Castle Hill was an island in the Pannonian Sea that lapped these shores; the flat plain on which Pest stands was under water. Lush foliage now covers the face of Castle Hill, once terraced with market gardens which served the houses and

palaces above. Logod was settled in the middle ages and was particularly famed for its luscious grapes - until completely destroyed during the Ottoman occupation.

Continue downhill now until you meet a busy main road - **Attila út**. Cross it and enter the tree-filled park on the other side. In mediaeval times this was a wide greensward field, where King Mátyás held jousts and feasting to celebrate his marriage to Beatrice of Aragon. Today the area is known as the **Vérmező** (Blood Field), so called because five leading Jacobins were executed here in May 1795. In the late 18th century a series of radical reading groups, inspired by events in revolutionary France, were organised in Masonic lodges around Buda and Pest, where they would meet to plot the overthrow of the Habsburg dynasty and the birth of a new Hungarian Republic. The movement consisted mostly of nobles, there being very few *citoyens* in either city at that stage, although it is strange to think that the educated nobility were plotting to do away with themselves. They were anyway swiftly and bloodily dispatched by the Habsburgs, who had already seen Maria Theresa's daughter Marie Antoinette (sister of Maria Christina) lose her head, and were not about to

let the same thing happen on their own territory. Turn left and walk through the park. It is worth peeping through the branches to your left to Attila út, where you will see sophisticated Bauhaus and Functionalist blocks, built by industrialists in the twenties and thirties as this area went up in the world. Before the war Krisztinaváros had its own casino, a summer theatre, and one of the best fencing gyms in the city. People who had not got the name to own property up above but had the fortune to develop land at the foot of the hill bought plots and commissioned architects of the Modernist movement. Attila út is, as a result, a fine example of this style; almost every other apartment block is designed according to Modernist precepts.

At the end of Vérmező you come out into Mikó utca. At the very end of the street to your left (on the other side of Attila út) stands a bust of Theresa Brunswick (1775-1861), lover of Beethoven and founder of the first nursery school in Hungary in 1828. The school was on the site of the white Functionalist block on the corner, now an estate agent. Estate agents are still a comparative rarity in Budapest, though property ownership is booming again. After 1948, when the Communist Party took control of the country, the people who still survived in these blocks had families billeted on them from the countryside and the suburbs. Families who had been living in spacious apartments suddenly found themselves sharing their homes, bathrooms, kitchens and hot water with perhaps six extra people. The houses were of course taken over by the state, and everybody paid a nominal rent; some for the privilege of living in their own homes. Today these flats are on the market once more as the increasingly old inhabitants (Krisztinaváros has one of the oldest populations in the city) die out and the "class enemy" moves back in.

Also on the other side of Mikó utca, on the right hand side, stands a **bust of Sándor Márai**, placed near the spot where his house once stood, a house that was reduced to a pulverised wreck during the siege of 1945. Márai writes memorably about his return to Budapest soon after, to be confronted with nowhere to live. Cross over and admire the busts if you wish; otherwise turn right down Mikó utca and walk down to the end. Here you will meet Krisztina körút, the high street of Krisztinaváros, always busy and noisy, full of fume-belching traffic and clanking trams. The fifties building straight ahead is the head-

1930s Functionalism on Attila út. This block is one of many like it that line the street.

quarters of Hungary's telecom company Matáv. Once a botanic garden stood on the site, giving way in time to a nobleman's palace. Some say the palace was destroyed in the Second World War, others maintain that it was pulled down before then because plans had been laid to con-

struct a German Imperial School on the site. Hungarians love a conspiracy theory.

Turn left into Krisztina körút, the fine, low-slung yellow house on your right, now the Theatre Institute, was once **home to Adam Clark**, the Scottish engineer who built the Chain Bridge (*see p. 30*), married a Hungarian girl and lived in Budapest for the rest of his days. Proceed along Krisztina körút now to **Krisztina tér**, the main square of Krisztinaváros. The school in dingy brick on the right hand corner may look more like a correction centre than a centre of education, but despite lack of facilities and sometimes draconian methods, the Prussian-style school system, which still prevails, has produced more Nobel prizewinners (*see p. 50*) than most small countries can dream of.

There has been a **church on Krisztina tér** since 1700, when a master chimney sweep erected one at the margin of his vineyards in gratitude for his family having survived an outbreak of plague. Today's church dates from the late 19th century. Count István Széchenyi, the anglophile moderniser of feudal Hungary (*see p. 17*) was married here in 1836. In those days, and for much of the rest of the 19th century and early 20th, Krisztina tér was an area of homely taverns and cookshops, a convenient halfway stopping point for wealthy Pest citizens making the annual summer trek to their villas in the Buda Hills. The Horváth restaurant on the left hand side of the street is now the only survivor, together with the café opposite the church. The Auguszt family first set up a cake shop here in 1870, but in 1951 it was taken away from them and nationalised. It is now named after an early 19th-century actress and entertainer: Mrs Déry (Déryné), born Róza Széppataki in a provincial Great Plain town, and married to a stern and disapproving husband who didn't think his wife ought to be on the stage. His disapproval didn't seem to daunt her. Painted Herend porcelain figurines of her with her little-girl ringlets and her guitar, once a staple ornament of bourgeois mantelpieces, now abound in the city's antique and bric à brac shops. The café serves good cakes.

HOLLYWOOD HUNGARIANS

Hungary has provided many of the famous names in cinema history, with emigrés flocking to the profession in their hundreds. The story goes that a sign was hung outside the Hollywood studios in the 1930s declaring: "Being Hungarian isn't enough; you need talent as well!"

BÉLA LUGOSI

(1882-1956) - Actor whose name has become a synonym for Dracula and horror all over the world. In 1927 he was cast as Dracula in a play on Broadway, and his mobile face and emaciated form caused a sensation. He went on to make films with glorious titles such as White Zombie, Mark of the Vampire, The Phantom Creeps and Night Monster. He always shrugged off his blood-curdling success as merely "a living" and lamented the fact that he was not taken more seriously as an actor. Little did he realise that he was to become one of the most famous cult figures of all time, with his name virtually becoming part of the English language. His life ended in a welter of drink and drugs.

MICHAEL CURTIZ

(1888-1962) - Director who worked a lot with the young Errol Flyn, making such classics as The Charge of the Light Brigade and The Adventures of Robin Hood. But his best known film must be the all-time classic Casablanca, made in 1942. He was amazingly prolific, shooting two or three films a year, and always stuck to tried and tested plots which usually relied on exotic locations or historical figures. He was also responsible for The Jazz Singer in 1953 and White Christmas in 1954.

ALEXANDER TRAUNER

(1906-1993) - Set designer who worked in France until the fifties, where he did the marvellous sets for Marcel Carné's Les Enfants du Paradis in 1943. His work on Orson Welles' Othello in 1952 won him awards at Cannes and made his name in America. Beloved by Billy Wilder, he designed many of his films including Love in the Afternoon, in which he also appeared, and won two Oscars for The Apartment and Irma La Douce. Towards the end of his life he designed Joseph Losey's sumptuous Don Giovanni in 1978, and Luc Besson's cult film Subway

ZSA ZSA GABOR

(1917 -) - Actor, famous more for her many marriages than her films. Her quip "Darlink I'm a perfect housekeeper. Venever I get divorced, I alvays get to keep ze house" has kept her on an endless round of TV chat shows since. Never boring, she starred in John Huston's Moulin Rouge (1953) and Orson Welles' Touch of Evil (1957), as well as Drop Dead Darling in 1966 with Tony Curtis, who is also of Hungarian origin.

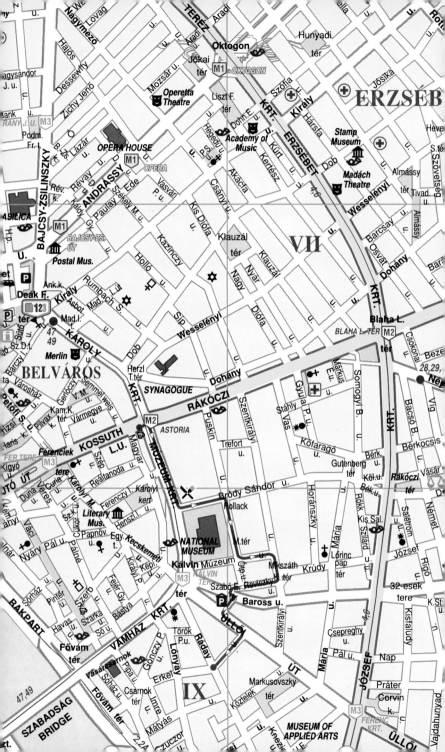

OLD PEST
OUTSIDE THE CITY WALLS

The best-known sights of Pest are predominantly 19th century - but a settlement existed here long before that date. This walk takes in the older parts of the town, including its mediaeval city walls and some of its former patrician palaces.

The walk begins in the coffee house of the **Astoria Hotel** (1912-1914), a fine chandeliered room with card tables and marble pillars and dainty Biedermeier chairs, where you can sit for hours over a single coffee and the waiters will never dream of pestering you. From here take the door out past the reception desk and into Kossuth Lajos utca. On the wall right above your head, behind the first floor balcony railings, is a plaque commemorating the fact that the hot-blooded young poet Sándor Petőfi once lodged in a building on this site. But more of him later.

A portly Kálmán Mikszáth dominates the square that bears his name.

Wise old owl outside an antiquarian book-seller's on Múzeum körút, one of the last-remaining neon signs in a city that was once full of them.

The Astoria has given its name to the busy traffic junction on which it stands. In the middle ages, one of three city gates stood here, leading out of walled Pest and onto the main cart road to the north-eastern town of Hatvan. The spot where you are standing now lies just outside the boundary of the old mediaeval city. Turn right and then right again into **Múzeum körút**. This road follows the very line of the 15th-century city walls. It is always busy with traffic,

especially in rainy weather when the whole system comes to a standstill. The buildings all along here seem stolid and workaday on the surface - but stop and look up at No. 7, designed for the Unger family in 1852, and decorated all over with a motif of eight-pointed stars. It is an early work by the later great architect Miklós Ybl (*see p. 20*), and the entranceway (open during working hours) still preserves the wooden cobbles which at one time would have been a feature of all these buildings (wood soaks up the noise of horses' hoofs and carriage wheels better than stone). No. 15 was the site of Hungary's first school for girls, which opened with fourteen pupils in 1869, thanks to the vociferous campaigning of Veres Pálné (Mrs. Paul Veres), one of Hungary's first feminists. From here, continue down the *körút*, pausing to glance down Ferenczy István utca. Straight ahead of you is a preserved section of **old city wall**. Walk on a little way and go into the courtyard of No. 21 (open during working hours), and you will see a particularly fine, battlemented section.

When the city was taken back from the Turks in the 17th century, the walls were never re-erected - but somehow their circumscribing aura remained. Only Catholics were allowed to build places of worship within the old city precinct; Jews and Protestants were relegated to the outlying areas. So it was that the area stretching back from the other side of the street from where you are now standing became the Jewish quarter of Budapest. The white building on the corner, with the restaurant on its ground floor, once housed the offices of the Holy Cross Society, a Catholic organisation that ran religious courses for Jews wishing to convert to Christianity. During the earlier years of the Second World War, Jews who converted were awarded government protection. In the last two years of the war, however, the rules changed. Adolf Eichmann arrived in Budapest in 1944 to carry out his Final Solution, and the Jewish quarter was barricaded with a makeshift wooden fence and turned into a ghetto.

Opposite to the right, behind the green metal railing, is the imposing bulk of the Hungarian National Museum. This was built by Mihály Pollack (*see p. 20*), one of the best exponents of Hungarian Classicism, and a member of the so-called Beautification Committee, which dedicated itself to resurrecting

waterlogged Pest from the disastrous flood of March 1838, which swept away most of the buildings in this area. The allegorical figures on the Museum's tympanum represent Pannonia flanked by Science and Art. It was outside the Museum building that the anti-Habsburg revolutionaries gathered on March 15th 1848, and the poet Petőfi recited his battle-cry "Hungarians Arise!". Fired up by all this, the people set off to

On the steps of the National Museum, the finest neo-Classical building in Budapest.

free the imprisoned Mihály Táncsics from the city gaol. Táncsics, a weaver by trade, married to a Budapest bootmaker's daughter, became a wanted man as early as 1842 for his radical pamphleteering: publications championing the freedom of the Press, the cause of the people, and Utopian ideals in general. With a price on his head he fled Hungary, but the Habsburg guard caught up with him in Croatia, and took him back to Budapest where he was summarily flung into prison. Freed by the mob in 1848, he spent the next ten years of his life in hiding, as legend has it, under the floorboards of his wife's house, behind a trapdoor concealed by a heavy painted trunk. Despite numerous searches and the tricky business of his wife having to explain away the mysterious birth of a daughter, he was never found, and lived to a ripe old age. Every year now, on March 15th, National Day is celebrated on the steps of the Museum with speeches and patriotic songs.

Cross the road now and turn into **Bródy Sándor utca**. Before the mid-

19th century this area was little more than a marshy stretch of cattle-grazing fields, farms and brick factories. After the flood, however, things began to change and the area began to develop rapidly, with wealthy patrician families moving down from the cramped, mediaeval streets of Castle Hill to the wider, purpose-built boulevards of Pest. Miklós Ybl was one of the architects to profit from this. He bought much of the land around the Museum, parcelled it out into separate plots, and gave building commissions to himself and his friends. One such friend was Antal Weber, who built No. 4 (1876). Eclectic in style (Weber's buildings

The wealthy chimney sweep who built himself a town house at Bródy Sándor utca 15 was not shy about how he had made his money.

were always either Eclectic or neo-Renaissance), with its Renaissance top storey and Classical Corinthian columns, this house is a rarity in that is built of real stone, rather than brick overlayered with stuccoed plaster, which is the case with most 19th-century Pest architecture. Weber was one of the most sought-after architects of his day - and brother-in-law of the noted artist Károly Lotz (*see p. 40*), who did the fresco in the loggia: Eros in a chariot with two cupids, representing the triumph of Love. No. 8, the neo-Renaissance **Italian Cultural Institute**, is by Miklós Ybl. Originally it was built to house the new Hungarian House of Representatives, which had come into being after the 1867 Compromise Agreement with Austria, and was where the Hungarian Parliament's lower house sat, before their vast bi-cameral palace on the Danube bank was completed (*see p. 142*). If you look up, you will see the crown of St. Stephen perched on the roof. The story goes that the local carpenters were put under such pressure to finish fitting out the building on time that they came out on strike. No hearts were melted; the problem was simply solved by importing alternative carpenters from Austria. There are plenty of fine façades in this street. Note the owl and the rooster symbolising night and

day on the balcony of No. 12. The façade of No. 15 is graced by the statue of a chimney sweep. The house was built in the 1850s for a master sweep who made a fortune from the grime of the city's chimneys. Bródy Sándor is also famous for being the street where the young communist activist János Kádár lived under an assumed name (the Communist Party was illegal at the time), as a lodger with Mr and Mrs Ottó Róna. Mrs Róna left her husband to marry Kádár some years later.

Turn right now into **Pollack Mihály tér**. This square was once filled with the town palaces of the nobility. Nearest to Bródy Sándor utca is the Arts University **Sociology Faculty**, swathed in wooden scaffolding, not because any work is being done, but because otherwise it would simply fall down. With all its wooden decks and planks and ladders, the building looks more like a 16th-century man-of-war than a town palace designed by Miklós Ybl for one of the country's Counts. When the main door is open, it is worth wandering inside to look at the magnificent carved stairway, now painted a grimy white.

In the centre of the square are the (mainly modern) headquarters of **Hungarian Radio**, with an ugly claim to fame: it was here that shoot-

ing first began in 1956 (*see p. 16*) after a storm of protesters had mobbed the building, calling for the freedom of the media. The Radio's third building, all of glass, stands behind a magnificent pair of iron gates bearing the proud crest of the Esterházys. To the right of this is the surviving part of the former Esterházy mansion, which between 1946 and 1949 was used as the Presidential Palace of the Peoples' Republic. Now it is used by the Radio. No. 3, the former Károlyi town house, with its grand carriage sweep, was designed by Miklós Ybl to look like a French country château. Gutted by fire in 1945, it has an unloved air today.

On reaching **Múzeum utca**, turn left. You are now in the heart of the area that came to be known as the "magnates' quarter". Múzeum utca was home to some of the grandest of the grand, including plenty who earned their riches rather than were born to them, and learned to live in a high style as a result. One such man was the fabulously rich banker Jenő Freystätdler, who purchased an aristocratic title as well as obtaining permission from his chum the Shah of Persia to style himself Pasha. His house on Múzeum utca contained statues of all his former lovers, coated in either gold, silver or bronze,

depending on how much he valued their memory. Walk along Múzeum utca now until you reach No. 17. This was the **town residence of Count István Károlyi**, uncle of Mihály Károlyi, the left-wing politician and architect of the National Council (*see p. 115*). István Károlyi, by all reports, was a famous *bon viveur*. A keen sportsman, he used to hold grand shooting parties at his country estate, and provide peasant girls from the neighbouring village to warm his guests' beds (one of these guests was Prince Edward, later Edward VII of England). After World War II his town palace was confiscated. "The revolutionary workers and peasants government" proclaims a plaque in the entranceway, "wanting to promote technical development, converted this house into a modern library". It still functions as a library today, which means that on weekdays the doors are open and it is possible to peer inside. Miraculously the front hallway has hardly been altered, and the magnificent spiral staircase and wooden panelling survive. Dating from 1884, they are the work of a Transylvanian master carver, of whom there were several operating out of workshops in the area.

Turn right at the end of Múzeum utca, and continue walking until you see the gleaming white statue of a portly **Kálmán Mikszáth** (a novelist, author of *St. Peter's Umbrella*, which was particularly admired by Roosevelt). Behind Mikszáth is a ruddy brick building with resonances of Morocco, perhaps, or is it Venice? This is Budapest eclecticism at its best.

With the statue on your left, turn right into Reviczky utca, and stop outside No. 6. This is the other side

of the Károlyi Palace. On the top floor you can see how the revolutionary workers and peasants government modernised the facility. In 1944 this was one of the houses where Raoul Wallenberg stayed, at a stage when he was constantly on the move, never staying in the same house two nights running, for fear of detection. A lot of the old aristocratic mansions in this area became safe houses, sheltering Jews and giving them diplomatic immunity. The eventual fate of Wallenberg was never known, the most recent theory being that he died in Moscow's notorious Lubyanka not long after the war ended.

Further down the street, the bright orange building which is now home to a music library was originally the town house of the Pálffy family, another French château-style creation by Ybl. At the end of the street on the left is a noble but grimy Rococo pile with a carriage sweep and intricate wrought iron gates (1887). This is the **Ervin Szabó Library**, once the town residence of the Wenckheim family. Seeing the way the political tide was turning, the Wenckheims sold their house in

The former Wenckheim Palace, now a library named after zealous Workers' Movement member Ervin Szabó.

the mid-1920s for a considerable sum of money - which they then imprudently didn't salt away outside Hungary in a safe foreign bank, so they lost it anyway. The library that their mansion now houses holds a collection on Budapest history and sociology, and it takes its name from fervent Workers' Movement adherent Ervin Szabó, promulgator of the teachings of Marx and Engels.

With the library behind you turn left into Üllői út, and then cross diagonally to the left into Erkel utca, at the end of which you will come into Ráday utca. This street has been semi-pedestrianised, and is a wonderful muddlesome mixture of old and new, with plenty of bakeries, cafés and restaurants all along its length.

WALK FOUR

OLD PEST
INSIDE THE CITY WALLS

This walk takes you into the narrow streets of the former mediaeval city, past Budapest's best inner-city park, taking in a handsome Baroque church and one of the belle époque's most literary of coffee houses.

The city of Pest in the 13th century covered a tiny area of around a tenth of a square mile, bounded by a thick stone wall. The oldest surviving parts of this wall date from before the Mongol invasion and sacking of Pest in 1241. When the citizens heard that the Mongol hordes were on their way, they apparently put up a second fortification to reinforce their wall in an amazing three days. All in vain, however. The whole lot was razed and the city ransacked. Two centuries later the Hungarians tried again, building more walls, this time with the added precaution of a moat and an earthwork. It still wasn't good enough: the might of the

Scene in the Café Central at the end of the 19th century.

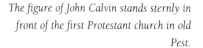
The figure of John Calvin stands sternly in front of the first Protestant church in old Pest.

KÁLVIN JÁNOS
GENFI REFORMÁTOR
NOYON.1509-GENF.1564

Ottoman Turks proved too much, and the wall was razed to the ground again.

.This walk begins in **Kálvin tér**, which stands just outside the boundary of the old city walls. Once upon a time this was an area of fields and vineyards and grazing land for sheep and cattle, scattered with simple mud-brick dwellings. In the great flood of 1838, most of those buildings were completely washed away. All that was left were the sturdier, Baroque-style houses, such as the little clutch that remain in the block nearest the church, with their steep, tiled roofs and plain shuttered shopfronts. One of these, the former Two Lions Inn, on the corner of Ráday utca, used to cater to travellers - one of them reportedly the composer Berlioz. Look up above the doorway and you will see the two lions still sitting there.

Kálvin tér is dominated by its plain, white church, topped with a spiked metal ball looking a little like a mace. In fact it represents a star, and denotes a Calvinist church. Catholic churches have crosses on their spires. This church was built on the site of a former Turkish cemetery, a plot of land granted to the Hungarian Reformed Church in 1801, a time when Protestants and Jews were not allowed to build places of worship within the official city boundary. The Calvinists were prepared to be patient, however. After getting their land, it took a full twenty-nine years until their church was finally consecrated. Opposite the church is the modern Hotel Korona,

occupying the site of one of the three medieval city gates, leading to the Great Plain town of Kecskemét, famous for its sandy soils and its apricots. This square is now, and always has been, a busy traffic junction. Formerly known as Hay Square, it was once the terminus of a horse-drawn railway that transported loads of hay to and from the east of the country. To cater for all the commercial travellers that besieged the area, inns and taverns sprang up, many of them of ill repute. As well as the Two Lions there was the Two Pistols, one of the most notorious. It was said by some that the reason it was so named was because unless you entered it with two loaded guns about your person, you were in danger of not getting out alive.

Kálvin tér is as full of people hurrying to and fro as it always has been, and to cross it you need to use the underpass. Follow the signs to Kecskeméti utca, which will bring you out directly in front of the Korona Hotel. Go underneath the green-painted archway that links the hotel's two halves, and into Kecskeméti utca. Immediately after the archway, on the left, is a red marble relief depicting a knight in

armour. This marks the spot where the old **mediaeval city gate** used to stand. From here turn right into **Magyar utca**. You are now right inside the old heart of Pest. Although nothing of the old mediaeval buildings remains, the streets follow the line of the original street plan, and are narrow and sometimes winding as a result. No. 28 Magyar utca used to be the Lamacs Inn, favourite haunt of poets and writers at the time of Hungary's struggle for independence

Consulting the morning papers in the Károlyi Garden, Pest's prettiest city park.

from the Habsburgs (1848-9, *see p. 13*). The most famous Hungarian freedom-fighter of all, Sándor Petőfi, patriotic poet and warrior, killed in battle at the age of 26, used to dine here frequently - on credit, we must assume, as he was famously penniless and couldn't even afford to paint the peeling walls of his nearby flat - and would declaim his latest compositions with inflammatory nationalistic zeal. On a less heroic note, this street was also the site of a notorious brothel, where a party of British MPs on a visit to Hungary in 1907 drank and debauched until the small hours - and then left the Hungarian authorities to pick up the tab. The Vintage Gallery at No. 26 is housed in what was once the Molnár and Moser Pharmacy - its old stone shopfront can still be seen, looking out over the **Károlyi Kert**, the Károlyi Garden, Budapest's prettiest inner-city park. The restrained and elegant town houses that surround it are typical of the early 19th-century style, plainer and more modest than what was built during the explosion of wealth and flamboyance in the years leading up to the First World War.

The Károlyi Garden originally belonged to the large house at its far end, the town residence of the Károlyis, one of Hungary's premier patrician families. The house continues a fine Hungarian tradition of nobility alloyed with ignominy and tragedy, however. It was from this house that Hungary's first ever Prime Minister, Count Lajos Batthyány, was dragged away into captivity in 1849. Batthyány, a nobleman from the then Hungarian town of Pozsony (now Bratislava in Slovakia), was pro-

The clean pseudo-Classical lines of the secondary school on Cukor utca (1913).

claimed Prime Minister of an independent Hungary in 1848. He held office for just six months. Condemned to death as a traitor by the Habsburgs, his appeal for pardon was rejected, whereupon he attempted suicide by stabbing himself with his own dagger. It was the gravity of his wounds which in the end melted the Habsburg hearts and led to his sentence being commuted from death by hanging to death by firing squad. At the turn of the 19th and 20th centuries, the house was the town residence of Mihály Károlyi, known as the "Red Count" because of his socialist sympathies. It was in this palace that he planned and organised his National Council, which governed the newly-independent Hungarian Republic after the collapse of Austria in 1918, and in which he served as Prime Minister. Károlyi was not popular with Western leaders, however, who found him too radical. In the event, in fact, he did find himself swept away by the power of his own reforms. When Hungary declared itself a Soviet-style Republic in 1919, Mihály Károlyi resigned. His house now contains the Sándor Petőfi literary museum.

From the Károlyi Garden, proceed down Henszlmann Imre utca to Egyetem tér. Straight ahead to your left is the Law Faculty building of Budapest's arts university, and next to it the **University Church**, one of the best Baroque churches in town. Under the Ottoman occupation, all the churches in Pest were converted into mosques, including this one. When the Ottomans were finally overthrown in 1686, this particular church was taken over by the Paulines, the only monastic order of Hungarian origin. The building that stands today is almost entirely 18th century, by Andreas Mayerhoffer, an Austrian-born architect who elected to become a Pest citizen. The beautifully carved main door is the work of a monk by the name of Brother Felix. If the door is open, go in; it is one of the most attractive churches in town (*see p. 74*).

Coming out of the church again, turn left down Papnövelde utca, noting the **secondary school at No. 4**, quasi-Art Deco with stylised Classicist elements - and architecturally far ahead of its time: it was built in 1913. Cross Veres Pálné utca now, a street named after one of Hungary's first feminists and a pioneer of women's education; it is perhaps ironic that she should have gone down to posterity under her husband's name, and her real name, Hermina Beniczky, is almost entirely forgotten. She died in 1895. Go into

The colourful dome of the University Library on Ferenciek tere.

Nyáry Pál utca now. On the wall of No. 11 to your left is a plaque commemorating **Katalin Karády**, who sheltered persecuted Jews in 1944. Karády, an actress and smoky-voiced singer of wonderfully slushy songs (available on CD), is Hungary's answer to Marlene Dietrich.

Retracing your steps, go along Cukor utca until you emerge at the **Centrál Kávéház**, which you will see on your right, with the yellow and red harlequinade cupola of the University Library rising ahead of you to the left. The Centrál was one of the landmark coffee houses in Budapest's great tradition (*see p. 33*), famous for being the place where Frigyes Karinthy, one of the greatest inter-war Hungarian humorists, first had the impression that trains were steaming through his head one March evening in 1935. "The trains started on time, according to schedule, at exactly 7.10. I clutched my head in wonder. What's going on? There was a definite rumbling, a forceful, slow screech, like when a locomotive's wheels slowly start off, and then accelerate into a noisy clatter... The train went past us, and ran on...." At first he thought he was going mad, but he turned out to have a brain tumour, which was later successfully removed in Stockholm by a famous Swedish surgeon. His account of this experience, *Journey Round My Skull*, deserves to be a 20th-century classic.

In the early nineties era of madcap westernisation, the Centrál suffered the indignity of being turned into a pinball arcade. Now restored to something like its former bohemian self, it is back in the business of serving good black coffee on an old-fashioned tin tray.

WALK FIVE

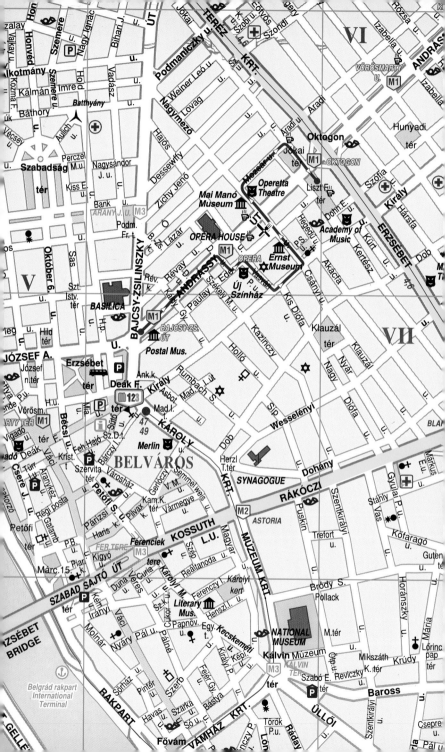

ANDRÁSSY ÚT

This route goes up Budapest's magnif-icent boulevard, a straight street that goes all the way from the city centre to Heroes' Square (Hősök tere). Visit a preserved 19th-century apartment, a splendid coffee house, and see the exuberant architecture of Budapest's theatreland.

"On afternoons of a fine day we may meet in Andrássy Street all the beauty and elegance in the city: it is a fashionable lounging place for the swells of the town and their admirers." So wrote Joseph Kahn in his 1891 guide to Budapest. And if Andrássy deserved a separate mention then, it definitely still deserves one today, being one of the finest streets of its period in Europe. It is a perfect example of the deliber-ate planning that went into late 19th-century Pest. Scores of one-storey houses were demolished to make way for it, and though at first the authorities grumbled, complain-ing that tasks like regulating the Danube and building landing stages and depots were far more important,

Andrássy út in 1896.

they were argued down, and work began in 1872. This dead straight street is named named after Count Gyula Andrássy, who was one of the few anti-Habsburg Hungarians to survive the 1848 revolution (*see p. 13*) and still make a career for himself. He went on to become Prime Minister after the Compromise with Vienna in 1867, and to preside over the country's much mourned Golden Age. Rumour has it that he had an affair with the eccentric, melancholy Empress Elisabeth. That is almost certainly a tale invented by hagiographers, wanting to ascribe passionate and noble feelings to an essentially self-obsessed woman. The fact is that she and Andrássy needed each other: Andrássy wanted to have one foot in Vienna, and Elisabeth wanted to vex her husband by being popular in Hungary.

Andrássy út is Budapest at its showiest and most theatrical. The Hungarian love of ornament is manifest everywhere: every available surface has received some sort of decoration: carved wooden doors, stained glass windows and ornate wrought iron gates were just irresistible to the nobles and wealthy bankers and brokers who commissioned the houses along this stretch. Unfortunately very

Neo-Renaissance caryatids flank the portals of one of Andrássy út's flamboyant palaces.

few of the buildings can be entered nowadays, and many of them have been irrevocably altered as old apartment blocks have been transformed into banks and offices. One building you can go inside, however, is **No. 3**, built by Győző Czigler (see p. 22) for a mineral water millionaire called Andreas Saxlehner. Czigler was well-known and much sought-after in his day; in fact this entire street was something of a showcase for architects during the late 19th century, and every house has a bronze tablet sunk into the pavement in front of it telling you who built it and when. These buildings may look massive and robust - look across the road at the bronze Hermes lording it over an eclectic confection of Ionic and Corinthian columns - but in fact the whole street went up in record time, as did most of 19th-century Pest, and all the ashlar and rustication is really plaster masquerading as stone. Although many of the buildings are now being done up, you can still catch glimpses of where the plaster is falling away to reveal the modest brick below.

No. 3 now houses the Postal Museum (see p. 48). If you haven't got time to go up and see it (though it is highly recommended, as the former Saxlehner home is well preserved) punch the number 10 into

the bell console and you will be let into the entranceway, which is splendidly decorated with frescoes by Károly Lotz (see p. 40), all with a mineral water theme.

At No. 9 two Graeco-Renaissance youths heave aloft the portals of what is now the **ING Bank**. Built originally in 1883 for the Brüll family, it was added to by Dutch architect Erik Van Egeraat in 1994. By glassing over the courtyard and placing a glass capsule conference room on the roof, Egeraat has managed to forge 21st century forms onto a conservative Historicist mansion. On weekdays you may go in and admire this spectacular transformation. A little further on, at No. 17, you pass the trendiest hairdresser in town, Zsidró. Fixed to the walls of Nos. 19 and 21 are plaques commemorating great Hungarian opera singers who once lived here. And if you look ahead to your left, you will see the **Opera House** itself (see p. 57). Many men had a hand in recreating Budapest in the late 19th century, but perhaps the most dedicated of all was Frigyes Podmaniczky. He maintained, a bit like Dr Johnson did of London, that one never needed to go on holiday because Budapest was a source of constant pleasure and amusement. He is even reputed to have affianced himself to the city

Art Nouveau mosaic and a replica bas-relief of King Mátyás's wife Beatrice adorn the entrance to the Ernst Museum on Nagymező utca.

when he was jilted by a lady love. He caught a hansom cab, and trotting up Andrássy út to the lake in City Park he dropped his ring in the water vowing eternal constancy to the great lady herself: Budapest. He worked tirelessly to modernise and aggrandise the Hungarian capital: before Andrássy út came into being, an inn of ill repute stood on the Opera House site, full of highwaymen and robbers planning fresh assaults on the good citizens of the town. One night Podmaniczky, enraged that this den of iniquity should stand in the way of his grandiose plans, stormed into the place armed with a cudgel, furiously knocking over tables and scattering the shifty clientèle. Not long afterwards the place was closed down and work began on one of Budapest's most spectacular buildings. Miklós Ybl who designed it (*see p. 20*) was the country's most celebrated architect in the late 19th century, and the Opera House is his masterwork. Historicist in style, he used Baroque and neo-Renaissance forms to create a building which is refined and decorative without being gaudy or insubstantial. The vaguely

erotic sphinxes at the entrances give the building an eastern touch - something which the great architect of the next generation, Ödön Lechner (*see p. 21*), was to rely on far more heavily. Lechner is responsible for the **former Ballet Institute** (1886), which stands immediately opposite the Opera and heralds the onset of entirely different preoccupations: here the emphasis is not on elegant Italian Baroque or Renaissance forms but rather on the mystical East, looking more to the middle ages for its inspiration. This was merely the beginning of what was to constitute a revolution in Hungarian architecture as Lechner slowly developed his ideas. The ballet dancers have all been moved out now, and the sounds of the piano and shouts of *"plié, plié, entrechat!"* will no longer drift through the windows, as the whole pile is destined to be turned into a luxury hotel. A century ago this was a famous café, the Reuter, a favourite haunt of stout, bowler-hatted gents with standing credit and a roving eye, who sat under its portals sucking cigars and libidinously eyeing the chorus as they came spilling out of the Opera

House. The only present survival of Andrássy's great age of the coffee house is the **Művész at No. 29**, just past the former Ballet School. Though tourist popularity has turned it into something of a museum piece, it still retains enough to allow you to imagine how it must once have been (*see p. 35*). In the summer you can sit out on the pavement, with the Opera House before you, and - almost - whirl yourself back to the 1890s. If you do decide to stop here you will have to retrace your steps afterwards, back past the Ballet School until you reach Dalszínház utca, where you will get a

The revue clubs of Nagymező utca have earned it the soubriquet "Broadway of Budapest".

view of the **Újszínház** or New Theatre at the end of the street. It seems appropriate that Ybl faces Lechner who then in turn gives way to Béla Lajta (*see p. 22*), the leading architectural light in the 1910s. This hieratic, geometric building was initially a nightclub, a sophisticated late-night drinking spot which is now a modern theatre venue with plays put on by directors such as Péter Halász, who ran the Squat Theatre in New York.

Turn left into Paulay Ede utca at the end of Dalszínház utca, and then right into Vasváry Pál utca. This street is named after a heroic student leader who died in the revolution against the Habsburgs in 1849, at the tender age of 23. People still commemorate him by placing wreaths on the tablet here. At No. 5 you will find the **Pest Lubavitch Yeshiva** (Talmudic college), started not long ago by American emigré Hungarians, though on the site of a former Talmudic centre. Tucked discreetly away in the courtyard is a century-old synagogue, one of many such semi-hidden Jewish places of worship to be found all over the city. District VII was (and still is) the Jewish district of the city, with a total of 35 synagogues or prayer houses. Today Judaism is enjoying a renaissance, and where once only a few elderly people celebrated the main holidays and even fewer regularly observed *shabbat*, there are now more and more people of all ages rediscovering their Jewish roots. This synagogue regularly draws a congregation of 150. Though the Lubavitch are a hasidic sect and observe strict laws, this synagogue and the yeshiva are open to the public, and as long as you do not disturb them on Saturday or Friday evening, you can go in and look round - if the door is locked, try upstairs, where the Rabbinical students pore over their books. English is the *lingua franca* here, so you are bound to find somebody you can communicate with.

At the end of Vasvári Pál you come to **Király utca**. Though Andrássy may have all the pomp and circumstance, it is Király where deals are done and undone. Originally the main drag in Pest, it was reviled by many of the 19th century's opinion-formers for being smelly, noisy and traffic-ridden. "Vile and narrow" pronounced the radical politician Lajos Kossuth, who heaved a sigh of relief when it was replaced by the elegant Andrássy - but Király still has a buzz about it. Turn left into it and you will see, at No. 35, an unimpressive second-hand electrical goods store - but if you go on a weekday the entrance will be choked with rakish fellows doing deals on beaten-up cassette

The Pekáry House on Király utca, one of the buildings that first brought the neo-Gothic style into vogue.

recorders and old fridges. This is also the street where you can eat anything from Syrian to Viennese and will see old traditional early 19th-century Pest houses still with their flowering courtyards next to grand mock Moorish structures. No. 47 a little way up from the electrical shop is the former **Pekáry House**, a magnificent crenellated concoction in burnt umber. Built in 1847, it was once home to one of the country's most popular writers, Gyula Krúdy, who wrote about the teeming number of people from all over the Habsburg empire who gathered in Budapest to try their luck and sell their wares.

One of the first buildings in the city to use neo-Gothic elements, it caused a small sensation when it was first built. From here, on the other side of the street, you will see the **Terézváros church**, built in 1801-11. It has recently been restored to its Maria Theresa yellow, so-called as Maria Theresa decreed that all public buildings throughout her empire should be painted this colour. The spire was designed by Ybl of Opera House fame. To the left of it is a little pedestrian walkway with benches, part of the city's regeneration programme to create open spaces and relaxation points for its citizens. If you choose to

Bistro café on Nagymező utca, one of a growing number of places catering to evening diners.

rest here you will probably hear music or scales wafting through the windows of the building next door, as this is the Bartók Béla Music School, which also has practice rooms for students at the Liszt Music Academy, which you will see later.

From Király utca turn left into **Nagymező utca**. This street, known as the Broadway of Budapest, is home to several galleries, cafés and theatres. This section of it was an artists' quarter at the end of the 19th century, and a number of plaques announce the artists' names and achievements. In No. 8 lived Adolf Fényes, who was one of the principle exponents of the Hungarian folk genre in painting (*see p. 39*) - his colourful still lifes and scenes of peasant life were a breath of fresh air after the heavy academic history painting that characterised much Hungarian art throughout the 19th century. Next door lies the **Tivoli Theatre and Ernst Museum** designed by Gyula Fodor in 1911. Ferenc Flau's Art Deco theatre lobby has been beautifully restored, and is worth wandering into even if you don't wish to catch a performance. The museum next door was built to house Lajos Ernst's extensive art collection. As a showcase for modern Hungarian art, Ernst enlisted Lechner to design the balustrade and the benches in the lobby as well as Rippl Rónai (see p. 43) to design the stained glass windows. Note the replica cameos of King Mátyás Corvinus and his wife Beatrice on either side of the main entrance. You can stop for a coffee or lunch at the Két Szerecsen, just up past the Ernst Museum on the corner of Paulay Ede utca. It serves light meals and snacks and is often filled with theatre people from the numerous stages all around it.

Cross over Andrássy út now into the other section of Nagymező, where at No. 20 on your left you will find the **Mai Manó House of Hungarian Photography**. This magnificent building was once the Arizona nightclub, patronised by swells and nobles from all over Europe, including Britain's Edward VIII. It was famous for its floor shows in the twenties, but its glory was doomed to die: its Jewish owner and his wife "Miss Arizona" were deported by the Nazis and the club was closed by order of the Gestapo. Today it functions as Hungary's biggest photo museum, with exhibitions ranging from the great old Hungarian masters (see p. 70) to contemporary photographers. Next to the Mai Manó is the plushly refurbished **Thalia Theatre** and opposite, at No 17, the blushing pink, splendidly neo-Rococo **Operetta Theatre**,

built in 1898. Operetta is something the Hungarians practically invented, and a night at the Queen of the Csárdás is a frothy affair of lost plots, mistaken identities and masses of ruched lace. If that is not enough, then try the revue at the **Moulin Rouge** next door. Recently reopened, it is worth going into the café merely to admire the Dante-goes-leatherette décor. Between the wars Budapest vied with Berlin for cabarets. The famous Barrison Sisters - a motley crew of cheeky soubrettes who passed themselves off as English, danced the can-can in flesh-coloured bodystockings and performed striptease routines on horseback - had every girl in Budapest imitating their hairdos and many a man telling fibs to his wife, plus one young nobleman blowing his brains out for love. The cabaret tradition is trying to revive itself, though it has been long buried - you only have to glance across the road to the huge blue and neon-bulb sign on the Socialist Realist No. 28, which announces the "18th Lawyers' Work Collective" to see how Stalinist design would have no truck with all that naughty nineties nonsense.

Turn right down Mozsár utca now and and walk up it into **Jókai tér**. Facing you as you enter is the Vörös Oroszlán (Red Lion) teahouse, a relaxing little place that makes a nice change from the endless cups of strong coffee. Glance down Jókai utca to your left and you will see the Buda Hills rising above the town in the distance, lending a sense of space to the densely-packed streets. At the other end of the square you come back into Andrássy út. The square is named after **Mór Jókai** (1825-1904), the Victor Hugo of Hungary, who scandalised the country by marrying a young show-girl at the age of 74 - although the statue of him sitting solemnly in an armchair gives no hint of this sprightliness. Cross over into **Liszt Ferenc tér** now, a pedestrian square given over to pavement cafés. On the right hand corner is the Írók Boltja or Writers' Bookshop, which has a selection of foreign-language books and Hungarian works in translation. You can either help yourself to tea from the samovar in here and browse through the shop, or pass on to to one of the many bars on the square itself. A frenzied statue of Liszt in the centre of the square (he is supposed to have regularly broken pianos by his furious playing) indicates the musical nature of this area of town: at the end of this long square stands the **Liszt Music Academy** (*see p. 53*). In the summer time, as you sit outside with your cooling drink, spare a thought for all the poor music students feverishly practising within its walls.

The prolific novelist and fervent Hungarian nationalist Mór Jókai.

WALK SIX

ALONG AND AROUND VÁCI UTCA

Downtown Pest is an appealing mixture of brand-name stores and forgotten streets full of ancient churches, fragments of mediaeval city wall, old-style beer bars and architectural masterpieces. Plus the city's best covered market.

This walk starts at the beginning of the southern section of Budapest's most famous pedestrian shopping promenade: **Váci utca**.

Broken in two by the busy road that leads to Elisabeth Bridge, this southern section tends to be slightly less crowded and more leisurely than the section on the other side of the bridgehead. Right at the beginning of the pedestrian section, on the right hand side, is a plaque announcing that King Charles XII of Sweden stopped here on his extraordinary breakneck ride between Turkey and

Looking through the main gates of the Serb church on Szerb utca.

Large-tile mosaic of St George, on the corner of Szerb utca and Veres Pálné utca.

Siraslund, a journey which he accomplished in just fourteen days in November 1714. Charles had found refuge in Turkey after the Battle of Poltava, which he had fought and lost against Czar Peter of Russia in 1709. During his time in Turkey he managed to bring the Ottoman Sultan round to his way of thinking and persuade him to join in the fight against the Czar. Peter, when faced with the might of the Ottoman army, was forced to conclude a peace and grant King Charles a safe passage back to Sweden. Charles refused to go, however, staying on in Turkey for another three years, until Danish inroads on his kingdom back home proved too much to bear, and had him riding like the wind through Hungary and Germany, back to a land he had not seen for at least five years. Charles came to a sticky end - he was shot in 1718, to be succeeded by his radical sister Ulrika Eleonora.

A little further up, at **No. 42** on the other side of the street, is a spectacular - if crumbling - apartment block built in 1908 in the emergent Art Nouveau style. Commissioned by a distinguished physician, Dr Sándor Korányi, it has owls perched up on the central projection, perhaps to indicate that this was the house of a scholar. Korányi's father founded the College of General Medicine in the mid 19th century, and was a colleague of Ignác Semmelweis (1818-1865), for so long the unsung hero of Hungarian pathology. Semmelweis isolated the causes of puerperal fever and campaigned to win acceptance for the use of antiseptics to prevent women from dying in childbirth. He realised that doctors were running from the dissecting room to oversee births without disinfecting themselves first. The medical world was hostile to his ideas, though, and Semmelweis died unlauded in a Vienna asylum at the early age of 47. Ironically the cause of his death was septicaemia. Within a decade of his death, however, his theories had become widely accepted, and he was being fêted as the "saviour of mothers".

On the right hand side at No. 47 you will find the **Church of St Michael**, designed by one of the foremost Baroque architects of his day, Austrian native-turned-Pest citizen Andreas Mayerhoffer. Originally it was built for the Dominican order, as the altarpiece with its romantic white-robed St Dominic with his characteristic black scapular suggests. The Dominicans received the church and adjoining seminary in 1747, but were to enjoy it for only a few brief decades. The Emperor Joseph II's 1781 Edict of Tolerance, aimed at weakening the power of Rome within the Hungarian church, sent them packing, and gave the church complex to an obscure order of nuns. The Edict of Tolerance closed down a total of 700 monasteries, but was friendlier to Protestants, allowing them the freedom to build places of worship where they chose. The nuns who received

this church were commonly known as the *Virgines Anglicanae*, the "English Maidens", after their foundress, an Englishwoman called Mary Ward, who established the order for teaching and charitable purposes in 1609. She and her nuns were invited to Hungary in 1628; thus they escaped the English Civil War and the later anti-Catholic legislation of Cromwell. The order was finally disbanded by the Stalinist regime in 1950, and the church and nunnery were only given back after Communism collapsed in 1989. The church is a fine example of Mayerhoffer's easy but decorative style. During the day the door is usually open, so you can get a glimpse of the Baroque interior.

Opposite the church is the headquarters of Hungarian fashion studio Manier. The balcony is often full of mannequin dummies and cast off hats. Favouring velvets, rich brocades and vampish silks, this young team recently had a splash in *Vogue*. Above the tatty shopfronts of No. 52 a little further on, look up to see a striking façade with colourful mosaics and folksy bas-reliefs. No. 54, in contrast, is a typical old Pest house, built around 1820. A plaque announces that this is where Béla Kovács, Secretary of the Smallholders Party, was arrested by the Soviets in 1947. Wreaths and flowers are often placed here to commemorate him. The Smallholders, who represented farmers and the landowning peasantry, were loathed by the Stalinist regime, who persecuted *kuláks*, or rich peasants, in the countryside, disbanded their politi-cal forum, and arrested and shot their leaders. Today, however, the Smallholders Party is flourishing again, and in 1998 it was elected a member of the coalition government. The next house along is truly magnificent in spring and summer, with its balconies of flowering

Elderly locals still sit and pass the time of day amid the teeming shoppers on Váci utca.

plants. In a city with a dearth of public parks, people love their window boxes, and in most courtyards in the city you will see pots of geraniums, oleander and even roses. This street was traditionally a residential area for city professionals, and many of the houses were commissioned by doctors, lawyers and bankers. Today the retailers are pushing the old professionals out, but this house still houses a lawyer's practice, an increasingly rare survival.

On the other side, at No. 59, is a plaque dedicated to Lipót Rottenbiller, who commissioned the building in 1847. Rottenbiller was mayor of Budapest during the 1848 revolution against the Habsburgs (see p. 13), and is regarded as one of the city fathers for the building and beautification programmes he initiated. His well-intentioned but dangerous ability to be wrong is generously overlooked. During a cholera outbreak in the 1860s he told the citizens not to panic, declaring that the disease was not contagious.

The great pile at Nos. 64-66 is the **New City Hall**, designed by Imre Steindl (architect of the Parliament, see p. 142) in 1870-75 as a place for the council of the newly united cities of Buda and Pest to meet. It still houses some of the city administration. Originally Steindl designed the build-

ing in the neo-Gothic style he so adored, but the policymakers of the newly-united capital, eager to begin their task of making life difficult, quibbled with the plans and reworked them in neo-Renaissance style. The result is the kind of eclectic theatricality that is so prevalent in Budapest. The next house along belongs to the Serbian Orthodox Church, as does quite a lot of property in the surrounding streets. Before 1914 Budapest was a mass of different communities; as the second city in the Habsburg empire it attracted people from all over that empire's dominions, as well as being home to German and Serb communities who had been here since the middle ages. The streets of the city would have clamoured with German, Serb, Croat, Slovak, Czech, Romanian, Yiddish and Ukrainian as well as Hungarian. Serb merchants traded here in mediaeval times, but the first great wave of immigration came when the Ottomans invaded Serbian lands. Great numbers of refugees came up the Danube, their possessions loaded into boats, to settle here in the early 16th century. Budapest was also one of the first points of refuge for those fleeing the recent Balkan wars, and Serbian is once again heard on these streets.

Turn left now, into the appropriately named Szerb utca, and walk

Old-fashioned trades rub shoulders with modern brand names in Váci utca.

along to the corner of Veres Pálné utca, where on the left you will find the lovely little **Serbian church** of St George, enclosed in its own pretty garden. Archaeological findings show that there was a church here during the Turkish occupation of the city (1541-1686), but it was destroyed and building only began on a new one in 1688 after the Turks had gone. Its present form dates from 1750, and it seems likely that Mayerhoffer was the main architect. The church can only be visited on Sundays during the service, which starts at 10am.

Cross Veres Pálné utca now, pausing to glance at the fey caryatids on No. 8, who are holding up an icing-sugar extravaganza. There is a great mixture of architectural styles in this part of town, from modest Classicist to frothy Rococo. Turn right down Fejér György utca and the architecture changes again. No. 1 is an old building with modern stone cladding on the upper storey. Opposite are some standard Functionalist thirties blocks. The CD-Fü bar in the cellar of No. 1 is a smoke-free, alcohol-free bar, very popular with students from the near-by university law faculty. If you feel

up to it, you can challenge someone to one of the board games that scatter the tables.

At the end of this short street you come to Bástya utca, Bastion Street, so named because it was the site of one of the bastions that studded the **old city walls** of mediaeval Pest (*see p. 111*). Straight ahead to your right there is an architectural dig in progress, and you can see how the surviving section of old city wall has been incorporated into the 19th century apartment blocks that now rise above it. Built in the middle ages to protect the city and demarcate its boundary, the walls also separated those with city and guild privileges from the poorer settlers who lived vulnerable without. The sieges and wars of the passing centuries have left almost no trace of the former mediaeval town. If something is not done quickly, not much will be left to posterity of so many of the 19th-century buildings either. The grimy stucco of No. 15 is falling away in chunks, and notices tacked to the wall at eye level warn drivers that they are parking at their own risk. On the other side of the road, at No. 12, an incongruous worker with handlebar moustache wields a hammer in relief against the ornate façade.

The exuberant Central Market Hall (Vásárcsarnok), built at the end of the 19th century.

At the end of Bástya utca turn right into Királyi Pál utca, and walk towards the traffic lights, past the old-fashioned Nana café on your left. This atmosphere of cheap penny boutiques, coffee shops and soup bars continues across the main street in Lónyay utca. Though the city expanded outwards in this direction in the 18th century, it was still pretty unknown territory to the respectable Pest citizen of the 1930s. The writer Antal Szerb wrote in 1935 that "no one knows about this part of Budapest but me... It is full of dirty coffee houses and shops giving off exciting smells". The buildings further along have a distinctly Victorian institutional feel to them. The style is open brick, and even when it is plaster, it is still brick-coloured. The building on your left is indeed an institution, the neo-Gothic College of Applied Arts, built in 1893. Turn down Gönczy Pál utca to your right, at the bottom of which is the **Vásárcsarnok**, the city's central market hall, which really is full of enticing smells. First opened in 1897, it was originally served by a network of navigable channels, so that barges laden with produce could unload direct to the individual stallholders. An international competition was organised for its design, and the judges awarded first prize to a team of French architects. But that was only the prize for design - nothing had ever been said about actually executing the winning plans. The building that was actually commissioned was designed by a Hungarian contestant, Samu Pecz. Inside the market, the row of stalls along the end nearest the river is popularly known as the *gazdagsor* (rich row), because it always has exotic produce out of season. Upstairs you will find a plethora of stalls selling fried fish and spicy sausage, served on paper plates with fresh bread and mustard, to be washed down with a glass of beer or a snifter of *pálinka*, strong fruit brandy. If fast food Magyar style doesn't appeal, there is always the Burger King just opposite the market's main entrance. This has the distinction of being housed in the former Nádor Hotel, a hostelry that was described by the early 19th-century English traveller John Paget as "the finest hotel in the Austrian Empire". How are the mighty fallen!

WALK SEVEN

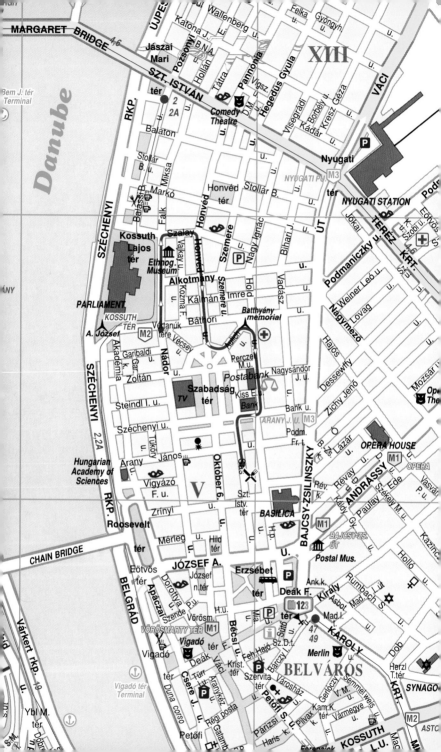

THE OFFICIAL QUARTER

Monuments to two revolutions against unwanted authority, Hungary's magnificent Parliament, and some excellent examples of the city's varied architecture are all included along this route.

This walk starts in **Vértanuk tere** on the corner of Kossuth Lajos tér, home to Hungary's grandiose parliament. This leafy little square takes its name from the *Vértanuk* (martyrs), thirteen Hungarian rebel generals executed by the Habsburgs in 1849 following the defeat of the Hungarian bid for independence from Austrian rule. The square now contains the statue of another doomed would-be reformer, Imre Nagy (1896-1958), who as Prime Minister led a bid for independence from Soviet-style Communism, putting an end to forced collectivisation and turning away from the dubious glamour of heavy industry. Disgruntled at this turn of events, the Soviet Union backed a coup to

Detail from Ödön Lechner's Post Office Savings Bank, a building which horrified many a worthy burgher when it first went up in 1901.

oust him. In 1956 Budapest took to the streets in protest (*see p. 16*). When the Soviet tanks moved in to crush the revolution, Nagy was offered sanctuary in the Yugoslav Embassy, only to be sacrificed by Tito, who realised that there was room for only one black sheep in the Soviet flock, and who wasn't prepared to jeopardise his own position to save Nagy. Despite assurances given to Nagy that he would not be hounded, the KGB arrested him and took him out of the country to Romania where he was secretly executed in 1958.

With the Parliament in front of you and Imre Nagy to your left, cross over Báthori utca and enter the colonnade immediately opposite. This building houses the **Agriculture Ministry**; the busts all along the colonnade commemorate horticulturalists, vets, animal breeders and agriculturalists who helped develop Hungary's rich farmlands. Built in a neo-Renaissance style in 1885, this was actually initially one of the competing designs submitted for the new parliament building opposite. On your left, as the first arcade doglegs into another, you will notice that the walls are dotted with small bronze balls, put there to symbolise the bullets fired on "Bloody Thursday" in 1956. But more of that later.

Cross the road now, to the immense **Parliament**, built by Imre Steindl over a period of two decades (1884-1904). After the Reichstag and the Palace of Westminster, this enormous piece of grandiose neo-Gothic froth is the third largest Parliament building in Europe. It is built right next to the river, on sedgy land, which had to be drained and stabilised before building could begin. When it was finally completed, the result was cruelly compared both to a Turkish bath and to a wedding cake - probably because, as it took so long to complete, by the time it was finally ready its ponderous neo-Gothic style looked hopelessly out of date in a city that was learning to relish the sensuous pleasures of Art Nouveau. Today it seems madly huge for such a small country, but in its day it was administering the affairs of the eastern Habsburg empire stretching from the Tatra Mountains to the Carpathians in one direction and to the Adriatic in the other. Inside the building, the walls and pillars are decorated with gold leaf above head-height, while within arm's reach the gilding is just gold paint, so that no one can profiteer from peeling it off. Numbered cigar holders line the window sills outside the debating chambers so that a smoking politician didn't need to

waste his good Havana when he went in to vote; he merely set it down in, say, No. 3, and relit it after he had cast his lot. Stained glass by the foremost masters of the time, including Miksa Róth (*see p. 47*), lines the corridors. 45-minute tours in English run at 10am and 2pm every day. The ticket office is beside Door X.

Continuing through Kossuth tér, a little further on from the main

Parliament entrance, you will find the **eternal flame**, erected in 1996 on the 40th anniversary of Bloody Thursday. On October 25th, 1956, thousands of people gathered in front of the Parliament to protest against the Stalinist regime. The Politburo panicked and snipers and tanks shot at the peaceful crowd. This only served to steel the will of the people still further, and gun battles took place on the streets until the Soviet tanks finally emerged victorious few weeks later. Much of the damage you see around the city does not date from the Second World War but from 1956.

On the other side of the road from the flame you will see the stately **Ethnographic Museum** (*see p. 45*) which was also a contender in the Parliament design competition. Along the balustrade on the roof are statues to Rhetoric, Painting, Geometry and the Arts and Sciences - the architect, Alajos Hauszmann, probably hoped that the MPs he envisaged within would be as cultured. At the far end of Kossuth tér is a gigantic statue of Lajos Kossuth himself, striking nationalist fervour into the hearts of ordinary

Statue of Imre Nagy, the Communist moderate Prime Minister condemned to death after the 1956 revolution.

Hungarians. A lawyer by profession and radical thinker by instinct, he provided the brains and the vision behind the 1848 uprising, while figures like Petőfi (*see p. 13*) provided the fire and the emotion. Kossuth was not captured by the Austrians, and so was not granted a martyr's death. Instead he fled to Turkey, from where he made his way to London, where he lived for a time, just off the Portobello Road. The story goes that he once stood up to address a crowd of British radicals, and spoke English with such an impenetrable accent that the crowd remarked how similar Hungarian sounded to their own native tongue.

Turn right into Szalay utca now. A plaque on No. 4 announces that it was built in 1939 for the Hungarian Chamber of Engineering by two pupils of Le Corbusier. The first four storeys housed the engineers, while the upper four were residential apartments, a fact reflected in the design, where the upper four levels have balconies with inwardly skewed windows. The plasticity of the forms and the calm mood of the whole is the work of János Wanner, who was part of a group who named themselves the "Little Robbers" after the restaurant they met in. Functional in style but Classical in its proportions, this building suc-cessfully blends in with the fussy Eclecticism which surrounds it.

Turn right out of Szalay utca into **Honvéd utca**, with its snack bars, baker's shop and cafés. On weekdays this area is buzzing with office workers, bank clerks and civil servants. It has always been busy. According to the essayist Sándor Márai, areas of town like this, that went up in the early years of the 20th century "were covered with clouds of dust. Building was going on on every street corner. The capital city of the great, rich, happy empire was having its image built, feverishly fast, and on a greatly exaggerated scale". Here, where before slum dwellings had stood, and muddy tributaries of the Danube had oozed between noisy, smelly timberyards and factories, tall, graceful streets began to rise up, as likely to be full of exciting, experimental new buildings as with template neo-Renaissance blocks. No. 16 on the right hand side is a wonderful crumbling Art Nouveau house with mosaics on its central projection and a prancing St George on the gable at the top. Apart from looking East for inspiration, the Hungarian Secession, as the Art Nouveau movement here was called, also delved into its folk culture, drawing on ancient legends, customs and traditional embroidery for its motifs. The

idea was to jettison all the historical styles that had been used until then - the neo-Gothic, neo-Renaissance and neo-Romanesque - and return to the village architecture of Transylvania, with its gables and steep turrets or the conical cupolas that are said to be inspired by the *suba*, the sheepskin cloak the herdsmen used to protect themselves on the windswept plains. At the end of the street, on the corner of Honvéd

utca and Alkotmány utca on the left hand side, is one such example: a short wooden spire and smaller hunting-lodge-style turrets rising off a building built in 1886, originally to house the Forestry Commission. On the Alkotmány utca façade you will find bears' heads above all the windows, and the ornamental entranceway features a male figure reclining against a log. Its designer, Győző Czigler, was to design a range of very different public projects around the city (*see p. 22*).

Now cross over Alkotmány utca, continuing on down Honvéd utca until you reach **Báthori utca**, named after István Báthori (1533-1586), Prince of Transylvania during the Ottoman occupation. He managed to secure a deal with the Sultan whereby he paid dues to Constantinople, but was largely left alone to govern his lands. He is also related to Elizabeth Báthori, the early 17th century "Blood Countess", who was walled up for purportedly bathing in the blood of virgins, although she was more probably the victim of a political plot devised by her son-in-law. Immediately opposite you to the right is a house with plaster peacocks over the entrance,

Aulich utca 3 (1901), one of the earliest Art Nouveau buildings in the city.

once home to Alfréd Hajós, who won two gold medals for swimming at the first modern Olympic Games in Athens in 1896. Trained as an architect, he designed a number of buildings around the city, including the National Swimming Pool on Margaret Island. Carry straight on down Honvéd utca until you reach **No. 3** on the left hand side. This newly restored building is a true jewel of Hungarian Art Nouveau, built by Emil Vidor in 1903. Commissioned by the art collector Béla Bedő, it draws on the international strands of Art Nouveau, using Jugendstil, Belgian and French elements mixed in with Hungarian motifs. Ceramic sunflowers adorn the balconies, with two bearded Babylonian figures above them.

At the end of the street bear left, and then turn left down Aulich utca, before you do so pausing to look at the green conical towers on top of the corner building on your right: examples of the *subas* mentioned earlier, and a feature you will see all around the city. **No. 3 Aulich utca** (built in 1901), its façade crawling with animal motifs, was one of the first Art Nouveau buildings to grace the city - look up to see the lovely glazed mosaic of a woman plucking an apple. At the bottom of the street is a little metal casket containing the **eternal flame** that burns for Count Lajos Batthyány, first ever Prime Minister of an independent Hungary. He was proclaimed Prime Minister in the anti-Habsburg revolutionary government formed in 1848. The following year the Habsburgs called on the Russian army to defeat the Hungarians, and Batthyány faced the firing squad in a barracks very near this site. Other revolutionaries, such as Lajos Kossuth, whom the Austrians hadn't been able to capture, were hanged in effigy.

Stop for a cup of coffee at the little café on your right. Otherwise bear right into Hold utca. A little way up on the left hand side you will come to the swing doors of the Vásárcsarnok or **Market Hall**. It is worth browsing through the stalls inside and looking at the newly done-up market with its ornate latticed iron girders and airy spaces echoing London's Crystal Palace or Les Halles in Paris. Once outside again, look across the road to Ödön Lechner's (*see p. 21*) masterpiece, the former **Post Office Savings Bank**, built in 1901. A riot of colourful majolica tiles on a façade topped by an undulating roof makes this one of the most spectacular buildings the city has to offer. Look for the winged serpents on the side towers, and the

engaged pillars which rise like tree trunks to the sky, complete with ceramic bees making for the hives of industry at the top. When it was built it met with considerable official resistance - somewhat reminiscent of the outcry that Gaudí provoked in Barcelona - and a decree was even passed declaring that public money was no longer to be spent on such radical projects. The building is now part of the Hungarian National Bank,

and you can walk into the small foyer and admire more swirling details inside.

Next door is the imposing, honey-coloured main building of the **National Bank**, remarkable for being one of the only buildings in Budapest where the stone façade is genuinely made of stone. The finely-carved reliefs that run all the way round the building depict the history of commerce and finance, either in literal or allegorical style - it is quite fun trying to work out what they are meant to represent. Follow the building round into Széchenyi utca, where on the opposite side of the road you will see the gleaming Bank Center, built in 1996 by József Finta (b. 1935), an architect who is responsible for a lot of Danube-bank hotels, none of which show him in a very flattering light. This, however, is a more successful undertaking, with its glassed-over atrium, a central glass pyramid and four towers all shimmering in chrome, polished marble and glass. It has an air of confidence about it which is in keeping with its function, though it has little originality. Right next door to it, on the corner of Széchenyi and Sas utca, is the former Financial Centre, a

Neo-Renaissance architecture is the most characteristic 19th-century Pest style.

Modernist mass with reliefs of wine-harvesting peasants on the far end. This was the first air-conditioned building in the city, and was both hailed and reviled when it went up. Today it lies sadly empty and forlorn, and no one is sure of its fate. Let's hope its asymmetric façades will soon be scrubbed up so it can vie once more with its neo-Renaissance sister opposite and its internationalist brother next door.

You have now come out into **Szabadság tér**. This square was once little more than a marshy wasteland, where the citizens of Pest would come to dump their refuse. The ever-zealous Széchenyi (*see p. 17*) drew up plans to fill it with trees, getting his wife to plant the first sapling. The anti-Habsburg revolution held up the programme of improvements, however. The square became more famous as the site of the hated *Neugebäude*, the vast imperial barracks where Lajos Batthyány was executed when the revolution was finally crushed. The barracks were torn down after the 1867 Compromise Agreement between Hungary and Austria (*see p. 13*), but the square was not planted with trees; instead, around its perimeter,

rose a sequence of grand public buildings, intended to be the organs of Hungary's partial independence. Most of them still survive today. Opposite you is the enormous former Stock Exchange, now the headquarters of Magyar Television, built at the same date as the National Bank (1905) by the same architect (Ignác Alpár).

To end this walk, turn into Sas utca, where the Café Kör at No. 17 will serve you breakfast, lunch or tea.

Detail from the fine stone façade of the Hungarian National Bank.

60 kg.

PAPIR

1 fa

ÉLETE

WALK EIGHT

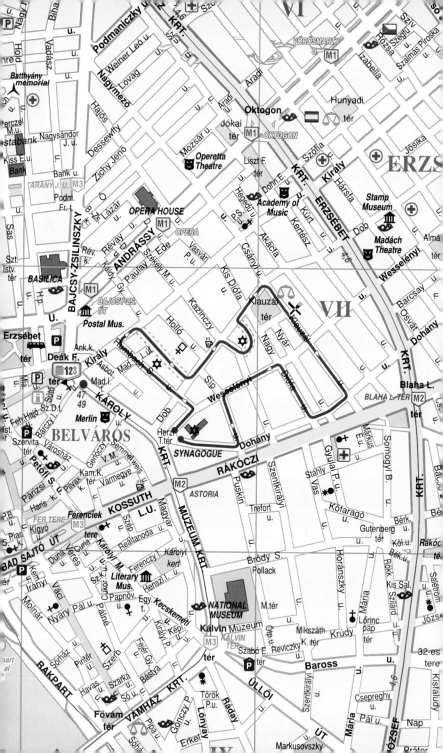

ERZSÉBETVÁROS

This route takes you into the heart of the Jewish quarter, with three splendid synagogues, a crumbling series of interlocking courtyards and a warren of old-fashioned sidestreets.

This walk starts in front of the **Dohány utca synagogue**, the largest in Europe, built in 1862 (*see p. 76*). It stands on the outermost fringe of an area of Budapest that has been home to the city's Jewish community since the 18th century. In a house that once stood on the site,

Theodore Herzl was born in 1860. Herzl has gone down in history as the founder of the Zionist Movement, campaigner for a Jewish homeland in Palestine. After the 1867 Compromise between Austria and Hungary (*see p. 13*), Jews received full recognition, and during the latter half of the 19th century the Jewish urban middle class played a large part in driving Budapest's burgeoning prosperity. Their tenancy in the main professions seemed secure, and the most obvious choice for

Orthodox Jewish children play in the Klauzál tér playground.

many was assimilation. Herzl thought otherwise. Writing to a friend in the 1890s, he maintained that it was impossible to be both Jewish and Hungarian; that in times of prosperity it might work, but that if times grew hard Jews would instantly be attacked and used as scapegoats - a prophecy not much heeded in those comfortable times.

With the synagogue on your right, bear up Wesselényi utca, where a small plaque on the synagogue colonnade announces that "Here stood one of the ghetto gates knocked down by the Soviet Army on January 18th, 1945". Just up from here on the right hand side is a small garden of remembrance, which was designated as a burial ground during the two-month existence of the ghetto. One of the most heartbreaking stones reads "Évike Bernfeld March 1944 - January 1945. By your birth you saved your mother and grandparents. We will always remember you". The wooden barricade that surrounded the ghetto was erected in December 1944, after Eichmann arrived in Budapest to put his "Final Solution" into practice. The ghetto was bounded to the north and south by Király utca and Dohány utca, and to the west and east by Károly körút and Kertész utca. Although anti-Jewish laws had

first been passed in 1920 with the *Numerus Clausus* (restricting Jewish entry to universities and white-collar jobs), and despite a series of more restrictive decrees that appeared from 1938 onwards, Budapest had a reputation for tolerance, and until the outbreak of the War acted as a refuge for Jews fleeing more oppressive regimes elsewhere in Eastern Europe. Although Hungary was a German ally in the war, Admiral Horthy's government tried to hold out against deportation. In the provinces he failed entirely, but Budapest remained fairly safe for a long time. There are even accounts of Jewish families holidaying by Lake Balaton in the summer of 1944, and of Jewish cabaret acts parodying Horthy and his laws right up until his government fell to the ultra-nationalist Arrow Cross in October. After that the deportations began. 600,000 people were murdered in the Hungarian holocaust.

Turn left down Rumbach Sebestyén utca - and be warned: this area is famously dog-infested, so watch your step! Continue down the street until you come to Dob utca. Look to your right and you will see, against a plain white wall, a **statue commemorating Carl Lutz** (1895-1975). Honoured by the Jews as one of the "righteous gentiles", Swiss

Consul Lutz had started the war helping German citizens who were stuck in Palestine, a British protectorate where Germans were regarded as enemy aliens. This meant that he was on good terms with the German authorities, and he used this to good effect by helping to organise passages to Palestine for Budapest Jews, as well as setting up 76 safe houses around the city. Lutz stayed on even after December 1944, when most diplomats left, trying as best he could to arrange papers and refuge. The Jacob's Ladder monument was put up in 1991, together with a quote from the Talmud, which reads: "He who saves but one man is as if he had saved the whole world".

Retrace your steps to Rumbach utca and carry on along it. You might notice a series of men pushing hand carts up and down here, as a few doors down at No. 10 is a paper collection point. Cartloads of used cardboard are brought in by the city's homeless in exchange for a few hundred forints. Just a little further down on the right hand side is a fabulous **synagogue**, completed in 1872 for the city's Conservative community. Designed by Viennese architect Otto Wagner, it is reminiscent of a Moorish palace. Although the building has been fairly recently restored, it is disused now and no

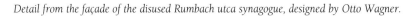

Detail from the façade of the disused Rumbach utca synagogue, designed by Otto Wagner.

one is sure of its fate. One idea has been to turn it into a Jewish study-centre and library; another (which the Jewish community vehemently rejected) was that Yoko Ono would buy it and use it as a rock concert venue.

Walk on past the synagogue, crossing over Madách út, and look left to see the **Madách complex**, a monumental mass of offices and apartments with a wide, yawning archway, built in 1937-40 (overall design by Gyula Wälder) as the gateway to a proposed boulevard which would lead right up to the Nagykörút. The project never left the ground, but the complex did, and remains incongruously massive in these small streets.

Carry on up Rumbach utca until you come into Király utca, and then turn right. In the early 19th century this was the site of a Jewish market, where a brisk trade was done in textiles, leather and wool. Nothing is

left of the market now, but the bustling character of the street remains. Go on a short way until you reach No. 13 on the right, and turn into the echoing corridors of the **Gozsdu udvar**. This forlorn series of interconnecting courtyards was built in 1904 by Győző Czigler (*see p. 22*), and was once home to a multitude of Jewish family businesses, Using German housing projects for

The Gozsdu Udvar, a series of interlocking courtyards between Király utca and Dob utca.

his model, Czigler placed seven interlocking courtyards over a long, narrow lot between Király utca and Dob utca, creating what was once a light, airy environment. It was a model project in its day, but now has been left too long to rot, and its future is very uncertain. All but a handful of families have been moved out of the dangerous, damp flats, and only the silversmith György Falk still plies his trade in Courtyard D. Film crews haunt the place, and everyone from Spielberg to Terry Gillam has used the space to create dark, sinister landscapes that are far removed from the original intention. Chained guard-dogs madly stand guard over empty space, and you will even see signs in Russian and Chinese, indicating some cold-war love story that was shot here.

Once out through the wrought iron gates at the other end, turn left up Dob utca. At No. 22 you will find the **Fröhlich café**, famed for its *flódni*, a wonderful wadge of walnut, poppy seed and apple. Family-run and very friendly, this kosher coffee shop is closed from Friday afternoons until Monday morning. Carry on up Dob utca until you come to Kazinczy utca on the right. Turn into it and you will see, on the left, the **synagogue of Budapest's Orthodox community**. Built in 1911-13 by the

Löffler brothers, it seamlessly meshes modernity with tradition. Designed to house a school, civic buildings, a restaurant and apartments, as well as a temple, it is now being restored and is very much in use. The inscription on the façade reads "This is none other than the house of God, and this is the gate of Heaven". Enter by the iron door to the right of the main entrance, following the sign to the Hanna Restaurant. You can peep into the synagogue itself through the small door just inside the gateway, and see its sky blue ceiling. The synagogue is only used for high days and holidays, and the Shas Chevra prayer house just inside the gateway to the right is what is used regularly. The gate is open from 7am to 3.30pm every day except Saturday, when it does not open until 11am. Go through into the courtyard and admire the stained glass at the back of the building, and the wrought iron *huppah* stand, or wedding canopy. Orthodox Ashkenazi communities hold their wedding ceremonies under the open sky, and the inscription is from Jeremiah: "The voice of joy and the voice of gladness, the voice of the bridegroom and the voice of the bride".

Walk on round the courtyard, and go through the Dob utca gate,

stopping to admire the Dob utca façade with its lovely Hebrew clock. Turn right into Dob utca and walk on until you come to **Klauzál tér**, a large park and playground where locals go to walk dogs, play cards and relax. Walk up to the top of the square and turn right. Halfway along this top end you will find the old covered market hall, built in 1897, and now occupied by a supermarket. A little further on at No. 9 you will find the **Kádár Étkezde**, a non-

kosher, Jewish-run lunch place serving huge portions of traditional home cooking (open Tues-Sat). A plaque on the wall further up commemorates Attila Gérecz, a poet-martyr of the 1956 revolution. He was originally buried here, and in fact Klauzál tér was a designated burial ground during the ghetto period.

Walk on down Klauzál utca now. At No. 17 an old bomb site now functions as a car park, a fairly common sight in the city. Many people remember returning from the war to find their apartment blocks no longer standing. Jewish writer Imre Kertész even recalls returning from the lager as a young boy to find someone else living in his parents' flat. When the Jews were deported people took over their flats, and not a few came home to find themselves displaced.

Turn right into Dohány utca and walk a few metres down, past the pot-bellied window-display of out-size gents' outfitters Mr XL, to No. 44 to see the entrance to the former **Hungária Baths**, with its languid bathers over the main door. Built in

Though the old market hall in Klauzál tér now houses a supermarket, impromptu stalls selling home-grown vegetables and home-made tomato juice crowd the entrance.

1909 by Emil Ágoston, who also designed part of the Astoria Hotel (*see pp. 101 & 171*), the building was bought by a bank in 1920 and merged with the Hotel Continental next door to become a fashionable spa hotel. The hotel building is now condemned, but the baths have a preservation order on them, although no clear future has been planned. Stories of Nazi atrocities carried out in the building during the war, when the empty pools were used as torture pits, also wreathe the building in further mystery.

Walk on down Dohány utca, crossing Nyár utca, and turn right into Nagydiófa utca. Before World War II this area was rife with small businesses. A zip-fastener repair shop is a lone survival in this street - and although the area still does boast glove-makers, milliners, cobblers and tailors, who all work out of tiny, street-fronted workshops, these old trades are fading fast as Budapest society becomes more affluent and throwaway, and as rents on shop space become more expensive. Turn left down Wesselényi utca. A shop at No. 19 proudly proclaims to be the last small-size ladies' shoemakers in the city. It is in an appropriate place, as the City Cobblers Guild was housed next door, in a wonderful mosaiced building built at the turn

of the last century. Turn left off Wesselényi utca into Síp utca, where the Jewish community headquarters are found at No. 12. At the end of the street, on the corner of Dohány utca, stands the glorious but dilapidated **Árkád Bazaar toyshop**, built by the Vágó brothers (*see pp. 22-3*) in 1909. The façade is adorned with reliefs of toys and of children playing. Crumbling and empty like so much in this part of town, it is now begging to be done up.

From here turn right into Dohány utca once more, and walk up to No. 10-14, a building which functioned as Budapest's University Press for many years. Now newly clad, it has been turned into offices and has lost much of its mighty Monumentalism (it was built in 1913). The loss of the press was a heavy blow, as it was the only printer in Hungary with the technology to print on the fly-weight paper necessary for prayer books and Bibles. Let's hope, however, that the new money coming into the area will have a knock-on effect for the whole district. Just past here you will find yourself back in front of the old synagogue again.

PART IV

PRACTICALITIES

FOOD & WINE

"Anyone who has had the fortune to travel the world, and who has tasted the cuisines of Vienna, France, Italy, Germany and England, will surely affirm that the best cuisine of all is that of Hungary." So wrote the head chef of Hungary's royal catering college in the mid-thirties. Well, if you like your food and like it rich, you might agree. The Hungarians enjoy eating, and they have a highly distinctive cuisine. One of the French chefs in vogue in the city today has airily remarked that Hungarian cooking will never be on a par with French cuisine unless it stops harking back to old fossilised recipes, and learns instead to adapt and experiment - but it is already beginning to do precisely that. A source from the latter decades of the last century was able to make the comment that "almost any (Budapest) restaurant of any pretension can boast of a French *maitre de cuisine* and assistant cooks of a different nationality, so that an Englishman is sure to find as good a roast or joint as his heart desires, if indeed he does not prefer to taste our national dishes in honour of the good wine". And it is interesting how true that rings today - well, not the roasts, exactly, but the foreign influence in general. The

burgeoning restaurant culture of the early 20th century suffered a paralysing setback during the lean years that followed the World Wars, but now Budapest is beginning to bounce back, with creative chefs and an increasingly discerning population. The new popularity of Mediterranean holiday destinations is perhaps creating too much obsession with rucola and frozen *fruits de mer* - but Budapest cooking is definitely in a transitional phase, and developments will be interesting to watch.

"Jó étvágyat!", Hungarian for "Bon appétit!".

HUNGARIAN CUISINE

Everyone has heard of goulash. What might surprise you is that in Hungary it is most often encountered as a soup. Rich meat and bean broths are popular starters, frequently made more calorific than ever by the addition of sour cream. Calorie count and high meat intake are the watchwords of the traditional Hungarian bill of fare. Frigyes Schädler, one of the city's owner-chefs, explains the calorie thing by pointing out that Magyar cooking is typically peasant food - and that means hearty stuff that fills you up and keeps you going in the fields all day. And meat, of course, was a luxury. Vegetables were for every day; steaks and cutlets were for special occasions, which is why restaurants offered them. But as Hungary becomes wealthier, fresh fruit and vegetables are coming back into vogue - a good thing, since a good climate and relatively unindustrialised farming methods mean that the produce is often a lot tastier than its anaemic cousins from the greenhouses of the west. Paprika, Hungarian cooking's other quintessential ingredient, first arrived in Hungary around four centuries ago, brought in by the Southern Slavs fleeing before the advancing Turks. In those days it was known as "heathen pepper", and God-fearing Christians wouldn't dream of eating it; they grew it in their gardens as an ornamental plant. It was not until the 18th century, when trade embargoes during the Napoleonic Wars made pepper unavailable, that paprika, cultivated on the sunny Great Plain, became the prime seasoning.

Some Classic Hungarian Favourites

BABGULYÁS: Goulash soup with dried beans. Usually featured as a starter, but with plenty of bread it makes a whole meal.

BRASSÓI APRÓPECSENYE: Small cubes of pork and potato fried together in a paprika sauce - a filling and full-flavoured meat-and-carbohydrate combination.

CSIRKE PAPRIKÁS: This is the dish that everyone's grandmother makes best in the world. Chicken pieces stewed with onion, mild paprika powder and sour cream.

HIDEG LIBAMÁJ: Cold slices of goose liver served in goose grease with toast and raw purple onion rings. French goose liver producers are allegedly up in arms that Hungarian goose liver prices are pushing them out of business. In terms of humanity to animals and kindness to your own cholesterol level, there is nothing to be said in this dish's favour. From any other point of view it is wonderful.

LÁNGOS: Deep-fried batter (yes, that is all it is) spread with garlic, sour cream or grated cheese - or all three. You can find a *lángos* stand at most markets, for example the one behind the Mammut complex on Széna tér.

PÖRKÖLT: This basically means stew, and can be made of beef, pork,

Blind walls are used all around the city for amusing trompe l'oeil advertising - in this case for Budapest's most popular brand of tea.

chicken or mutton. It is supposed to be eaten with *galuska*, the Hungarian non-potato version of gnocchi. Waiters may even gently suggest that you've made a mistake if you ask to have it with potato.

SOMLÓI GALUSKA: Sponge squares soaked in brandy, scattered with raisins and mixed with whipped cream and rich chocolate sauce.

SZTRAPACSKA & TÚRÓS CSUSZA: In traditional restaurants, these may well be featured on the dessert menu. The first is a combination of pasta, curd cheese, sour cream and crisp-fried cubes of pork fat. The second is pretty much the same idea.

TÖLTÖTT KÁPOSZTA: Savoy cabbage leaves stuffed with rice and minced pork, flavoured with savory, and served on a bed of sauerkraut in paprika sauce, crowned with a spicy sausage and a curl of pork fat, plus liberal dollops of sour cream.

For a selection of recommended restaurants, see p. 166.

Paprika, the classic Hungarian seasoning, is not in fact indigenous to the region, but was introduced by the Southern Slavs in the 16th century.

WINE

If your palate has been conditioned by the full-fruit flavours of Californian or Australian vintages, you might find that Hungarian wines take some getting used to. Even so, there is no doubt that excellent wine is being produced here, and Hungary can be proud of its viticultural traditions. Admittedly, Hungary is now drifting more towards the mainstream, with more and more noble grape varieties being used. But the native varieties are still hanging on, with a number of winemakers taking a definitive stand in their favour. High-acid Hungarian whites and light, spicy reds do not necessarily complement the Mediterranean-style cooking that is all the rage in the wealthier parts of the country, but they are excellent with traditional spicy sausage and paprika-rich stews, and it would be a mistake to sacrifice them on the altar of global trend. Summers here are hot, but not blistering, and winters are cold - which makes Hungary, not surprisingly, predominantly a white wine producer. If you are interested in going into detail on the wine subject, visit the Magyar Borok Háza on Fortuna utca on Castle Hill. A huge cellar space has been given over to displays from all the wine regions, with open bottles of selected vintages for visitors to sample. For expert advice on what to buy, you need to visit a specialist shop. Two good ones are the Bortársaság cellar at Batthyány utca 59 in Buda, and La Boutique des Vins at József Attila utca 12 in Pest. Hungary has around twenty official wine regions, of which the best are:

VILLÁNY: In the south of the country, it produces Hungary's heartiest reds. Winemakers to look out for are Attila Gere and József Bock in the premier league, with Mayer, Günzer, Vylyan and Wunderlich coming up behind them. Some of the top producers use a lot of new oak during the ageing process. If you aren't a fan of that, try the region's indigenous *Kékoportó* (Blauportugieser), a soft, fruity wine for drinking rather than for cellaring.

EGER: In the north-east of the country, famous for its red Bull's Blood (*Bikavér*), a light and spicy blend which became popular as a safe alternative to cholera-infested water in the early nineteenth century. Winemakers to look out for are Vilmos Thummerer, István Tóth, Tamás Pók and Endre Bakondi.

SZEKSZÁRD: To the south of Budapest, this is the home of light reds best drunk with food, and there is also a Szekszárd version of Bull's Blood, which locals claim springs from an older tradition than that of Eger. Winemakers to look out for are Ferenc Vesztergombi, Ferenc Takler and Tamás Dúzsi, who makes a good *Kékfrankos* (light, peppery red) and a lovely, summery rosé.

BALATON: Vineyards have been planted on the shores of this great lake since Roman times. It is primarily a white wine region, producing a lot of unfashionable (though often very good) Italian Riesling and some Chardonnay, along with Traminer, Sauvignon Blanc and Pinot Gris. The northern shore of the lake is volcanic, with a soil rich in acids, making for some interesting wines. Good winemakers are Huba Szeremley (Szent Orbán Pince), Ottó Légli and Mihály Figula.

SOMLÓ: Hungary's smallest wine region, tiny and compact, clinging to the slopes of an extinct volcano, and producing white wine only. The volcanic soil here is even richer in acids and minerals than north Balaton soil, which means that traditionally "flowery" varieties like Traminer taste much bolder. Produces plenty of the traditional Hungarian varieties *Hárslevelű* and *Furmint*. Allegedly

Somló wine was administered to Habsburg brides to ensure the production of a male heir. Winemakers to look out for are Imre Györgykovács and Béla Fekete.

TOKAJ

Undoubtedly Hungary's most famous wine region - more rubbish and more true words have been spoken and printed about it than about any other. What most people mean when they talk about "Tokaj wine" is *Tokaji Aszú*, an aged dessert wine made from adding berries infected by the noble rot *botrytis cinerea* to the base wine. The botrytis shrivels the grapes and gives them a certain flavour and sweetness. Traditionally the *aszú* berries were

added to the other grapes by the hod, or *puttony*. Technology and instinct have supplanted the *puttony* now, but the word is still used as a measure of sweetness. The higher the *puttony* number the sweeter - and pricier - the wine. The lowest *puttony* number is 3 and the highest is 6, though not every year yields enough botrytised grapes to make a 6-*puttony* wine, and increasingly 3-*puttony* wines are being marketed as "noble late harvest" or some appellation which sounds less bottom-of-the-scale. Vast sums of money have been spent by the French, British and Spanish on buying Tokaj wineries, and small individual growers and wine-makers are also coming to the fore. Some say the *aszú* wine is better since the so-called post-Communist Tokaj Renaissance; others like it less. This is something you can only judge for yourself. Good years for old-style *Tokaji Aszú* are 1972, 1975, 1983 and 1988, and, for the new style, 1993, 1995 and 1996. Top private producers of *Aszú* are István Szepsy, Gergely Vincze (Úri Borok), and Marta Wille-Baumkauff. The best of the large, internationally-owned wineries are Hétszőlő, Disznókő and Oremus.

The term "Tokaj" can otherwise be used either to mean any white wine made in the region, but typically from the native grape varieties *Furmint* and *Hárslevelű*; or *Tokaji Szamorodni*. *Szamorodni* is more akin to sherry, and takes its name from a Polish word meaning "as it comes", because the grapes are fermented together unsorted: some bunches will have more *aszú* berries, some fewer. As a result of this, the wine can be either sweet or dry.

RESTAURANTS

This is an entirely personal selection of restaurants to reflect the current dining scene in Budapest. Some places have been chosen for their food; others for the way they look, for their atmosphere, and for what they tell you about contemporary Budapest.

For a fuller listing of restaurants, check the publications given on p. 174, or look on www.inyourpocket.com

Key to pricing:
$ = cheap (around 5,000 Ft for two)
$$ = moderate (up to 10,000 Ft for two)
$$$ = moderately expensive (up to 20,000 Ft for two)
$$$$ = expensive (20,000 Ft or over for two)

NB: Though most places in Budapest now take credit cards, it is always prudent to take cash just in case. Smaller places may accept cash only.

HUNGARIAN CUISINE

ALABÁRDOS

Buda I, Országház utca 2. Tel: 356-0851. Noon-4pm & 7pm-11pm Mon-Sat. $$$$
One of the better restaurants on Castle Hill - for such a prime location it is a shame that so few of them are worth visiting. Fun in summer when you can sit out in the mediaeval arcaded courtyard. Slightly fussy service but good food and wine, plus seasonal specials. Live guitar music. Not many locals.

GUNDEL

Pest XIV, Állatkerti út 2. Tel: 321-3550. Noon-4pm & 6.30pm-midnight every day.
$$$$
Founded in 1894, this is Budapest's premier restaurant, serving time-honoured Hungarian fare in glittering surroundings. Food does not always live up to the promise of the atmosphere, but it's still a place worth dressing up for. Very good gypsy band. Garden in summer.

HORGÁSZTANYA

Buda I, Fő utca 27. Noon-11pm every day.
$
This place has made no concessions to changing tastes and fashion. It still retains all the characteristics of a typical Buda tavern: slighty dingy and

lent carpaccio and tiramisu. Freshly-squeezed orange juice and home-made lemonade. Street terrace in summer. A popular favourite.

CAFÉ KÖR

Pest V, Sas utca 17. Tel: 311-0053. 10am-10pm Mon-Sat. $$

Good-looking, lively bistro-style restaurant interpreting Hungarian cuisine for international tastes, plus classic Magyar puddings such as *mákos guba*, a sort of sugary concoction of bread, milk and poppy seeds. Popular with locals and expatriates, jolly atmosphere. Booking essential.

CHAPTER ONE

Pest V, Nádor utca 29. Tel: 354-0113. Open until midnight every day. $$$

This place has more than a whiff of nineties London or Barcelona. Very stylish, with clientèle and a menu to match. A place to see and be seen, with a genial proprietor who greets customers as they arrive. Large bar area where you can lounge with a cocktail before going to your table.

KÉT SZERECSEN

Pest VI, Nagymező utca 14. Tel: 343-1984. 8am-1am Mon-Fri; 11am-1am Sat-Sun. $$

Attractive but smoky bistro bar, with Mediterranean-inspired salads and grilled meats and a good choice of wines.

LOU LOU

Pest V, Vigyázó Ferenc utca 4. Tel: 312-4505. Noon-3pm & 7pm-midnight Mon-Fri, Sat 6pm-midnight. $$$

Stylish restaurant with an international feel. Good for a leisurely lunch or elegant dinner. Cuisine is French-inspired without being truly French, and includes dishes such as duck à l'orange with chocolate sauce. Booking essential.

RIVALDA

Buda I, Színház utca 5-9. Tel: 489-0236. 11.30am to 11.30 pm every day. $$

Almost the only restaurant on Castle Hill that is patronised by locals. Good varied menu, a sort of Magyar-Mediterranean fusion. Very pretty inner courtyard in summer, part of what was formerly a nunnery.

VÖRÖS ÉS FEHÉR

Pest VI, Andrássy út 41. Tel: 413-1545. Open noon-midnight Mon-Sat. $$$

Budapest's only wine bar, with a selection of vintages to sample by the glass, and tapas to taste with them. Also doubles as a restaurant, with tasty, inventive cuisine. Lively, youthful atmosphere in the evenings. Quieter at lunchtime. Its location makes it a good choice for dinner after the Music Academy or Opera.

grubby, with waiters who make no attempt to charm, but serving some of the best fish soup (halászlé) in town. Especially good is the korhely halászlé.

KÁRPÁTIA
Pest V, Ferenciek tere 7-8. Tel: 317-3596. 11am-11pm every day. $$$
Magnificent old restaurant, with not an inch of space left ungilded or undecorated, in a neo-Gothic style reminiscent of the Mátyás Church. The best dishes are the traditional staples such as stuffed cabbage or the soups and stews (pörkölt). Good goose liver. Most of the other dishes are rather ordinary. Gypsy band in the evenings. Beer bar area with a more informal feel. Candlelit terrace in summer.

KÜLVÁROSI KÁVÉHÁZ
Pest IV, István út 26. Tel: 379-1568. 8am-midnight every day. $$
Informal and fun out-of-town mock recreation of a belle époque bourgeois salon. Café section and restaurant section. The latter has live piano in the evenings. Cuisine is mainly Hungarian, with good steaks. Friendly service.

MÚZEUM KÁVÉHÁZ
Pest VIII, Múzeum körút 12. Tel: 338-4221. Noon-1am Mon-Sat. $$$
High, echoing restaurant, can feel a little barn-like despite the aimed-for grandeur, but the ceilings are beauti-

ful (frescoes by Károly Lotz, see p. 40) and the food very Magyar, though "continental" dishes are also making a showing.

NÁNCSI NÉNI
Buda II, Ördögárok út 80. Tel: 397-2742. Noon-11pm every day. $$
Out-of-town taverns were once a Buda speciality. This family-style place aims to prolong the tradition with good old Hungarian recipes, and tables in the garden in the summer. Booking essential.

INTERNATIONAL CUISINE

ARCADE
Buda XII, Kiss János Altábornagy utca 38. Tel: 225-1969. 11am-11pm Tues-Sun. $$$
Popular haunt for Budapest's new breed of trendsetters in a primarily residential area. Careful attention has been paid to both decor and the menu, which is short but with something for everyone. Slick service. Imbued with a distinct feeling of success. Tends to get smoky by the end of the evening.

CAFÉ GUSTO
Buda II, Frankel Leó út 12. Tel: 316-3970. 10am-10pm Mon-Sat. $$
Tiny, intimate café bar serving cold food only. Good pasta salads; excel-

OTHER CUISINES

CHEZ DANIEL

Pest VI, Szív utca 32. Tel: 302-4039.
Noon-3pm & 7pm-11pm every day. $$$
Talented owner-chef from the
Ardèche firmly stamps his personali-
ty on this family restaurant. On a
good day, food here is superb.
Leisurely service - don't come here
on a tight schedule. Very pretty
inner-courtyard terrace in summer.
Booking essential.

LE JARDIN DE PARIS

Buda 1, Fő utca 20. Tel: 201-0047. Noon-
midnight every day. $$$
Nice interior, filled with 1920s
prints. Food and service can be
erratic (the lamb Provençale is usually good), but it boasts the most beautiful garden in the summer.

FAUSTO'S

Pest VII, Dohány utca 5. Tel: 269-6806.
Noon-3pm & 7pm-midnight Mon-Sat.
$$$$
Enduringly popular with a predominantly business clientele. Resolutely
stylish, serving Italian 'haute cuisine'. Booking essential.

KRIZIA

Pest VI, Mozsár utca 12. Tel: 331-8711.
Noon-3pm & 6.30-midnight Mon-Sat. $$$
Talented chef from Bergamo com-

bines a warm, relaxed atmosphere
with some of the best cooking in
Budapest. Everything always fresh
and in season. Stunning truffle risot-
to. Booking recommended.

ARANY KAVIÁR

Buda I, Ostrom utca 19. Tel: 201-6737.
6pm-midnight every day. $$$
Ice-cold vodka, a choice of caviar,
and classic Russian specials such as
Volga sturgeon and *pirog* (liver and
boeuf *en croute*) cooked up by smil-
ing chef Sasha. Lighter meals also on
offer.

AL AMIR

Pest VII, Király utca 17. Tel: 352-1422.
11am-11pm Mon-Sat; 1.30pm-11pm Sun. $
Syrian restaurant with delicious pastries and light bites for lunch. Good
hummus and aubergine dips served
with hot pitta bread. Peaceful and
informal. No alcohol.

VEGETARIAN

GANDHI

Pest V, Vigyázó Ferenc utca 4. Tel: 269-
4944. Noon-10pm every day. $$
Slightly New Agey, non-smoking
restaurant, with a variety of fresh
salads, plus vegetarian and vegan
dishes.

HOTELS &
ACCOMMODATION

HOTELS

This list is not exhaustive. It is a subjective selection, giving a cross-section of the kind of hotel accommodation Budapest has to offer. Smaller-scale, privately-run hotels of charm are sadly a category that does not exist in the Hungarian capital. A fuller list can be found on www.inyourpocket.com

Postal districts are given in all cases (Roman numerals). Telephone numbers are Budapest, code (06)1 from inside Hungary or +361 from abroad.

Approximate price guides are as follows, for a regular double or twin room per night, excluding local tax:
$: under $100
$$: $100-150
$$$: $150-200
$$$$: over $200

The lounge of Le Meridien.

LUXURY HOTELS

HILTON BUDAPEST
Built in the 1970s on the remains of a mediaeval monastery, this is now a typical luxury chain hotel: fitted carpets, piped music, not much individual character but every comfort. The Castle Hill location is a big plus.
322 rooms. $$$$
Buda I, Hess András tér 1-3
Tel: 488-6600; Fax: 488-6925
www.hilton.com

INTER-CONTINENTAL
Decorated in the Inter-Continental corporate style. Unprepossessing from the outside, but boasts an excellent Danube-bank location, as well as the best panoramic views in Budapest, across the Danube and Chain Bridge to Castle Hill. Swimming pool and fitness centre.
398 rooms. $$$$
Pest V, Apáczai Csere János utca 12-14
Tel: 327-6333; Fax: 327-6357
www.interconti.com

Kempinski Hotel Corvinus

Classic international luxury hotel with a businessy flavour to it in a well-designed modern building right in the centre of Pest. Clean and comfy and professional. Swimming pool and health centre.

369 rooms. $$$$

Pest V, Erzsébet tér 7-8

Tel: 429-3777; Fax: 429 4777

www.kempinski-budapest.com

Le Meridien

Cool, tasteful French Empire-style decor, very comfortable rooms. Completely renovated early 20th-century building in central Pest. The aim is to recreate old-fashioned gracious living, not to be modern or funky. French pastry chef lays out wonderful afternoon teas. Swimming pool and health centre.

218 rooms. $$$$

Pest V, Erzsébet tér 9-10

Tel: 429-5500; Fax: 429-5555

www.lemeridien-budapest.com

Medium-Range Hotels

Art'Otel

Filled with contemporary art by Donald Sultan, this hotel is an intriguing mix of 1990s modern and early 18th-century Buda Baroque. Rooms on the front have good Danube views; rooms in the old, stone-built section

Main entrance of the Kempinski Hotel.

on the other side are cooler and quieter. All are decorated with a predominance of bright red.

165 rooms. $$$

Buda I, Bem rakpart 16-19

Tel: 487-9487; Fax: 487-9488

www.parkplazaww.com

Astoria

Elegant, early 20th-century public rooms with lots of gilt and green marble, survivals of Budapest's belle époque. Bedrooms are a bit disappointing but adequate. Situated on a busy central crossroads, so ask for a room at the back.

131 rooms, both double and twin - specify what you want. $$

Pest V, Kossuth Lajos utca 19-21

Tel: 484-3200; Fax: 318-6798
www.danubiusgroup.com/astoria

Tel: 269-0222; Fax: 269-0230
www.kkhotels.com

GELLÉRT

One of Budapest's classics, attached to the Art Nouveau Gellért thermal baths. Most of the main rooms have a slightly 70s flavour, but the hotel is comfortable and well-run. Use of baths included in room rate.
234 rooms. $$
Buda XI, Szent Gellért tér 1
Tel: 385-2200; Fax: 466-6631
www.danubiusgroup.com/gellert

VICTORIA

Small, privately-run modern hotel on the Danube bank in Buda. All rooms are front-facing, with views of the river. The decor is rather dated, but the hotel is friendly and its small size is a big point in its favour.
27 rooms. $
Buda I, Bem rakpart 11
Tel: 457-8080; Fax: 457-8088
www.victoria.hu

K+K HOTEL OPERA

Light, bright modern decor: clean lines, lots of wicker, and a definite preference for sunflower yellow. Good central Pest location, right by the Opera House. Baby-sitter service.
205 rooms. $$
Pest VI, Révay utca 24

BASIC BUT FUN

BURG HOTEL

Small modern hotel on Castle Hill, with views of the Mátyás Church. Rooms at the back look onto an old section of city wall. Rooms basic but functional.

Stunning Danube views from the Intercontinental.

The Chelsea restaurant in the Art'Otel, by the Danube in Buda.

26 rooms. $
Buda I, Szentháromság tér
Tel: 212-0269; Fax: 212-3970
e-mail: hotel.burg@mail.datanet.hu

KULTURINNOV

A hotel of great character: early 20th-century neo-Gothic twinned with basic Communist-era make-do and mend functionalism. No TV sets in the rooms, which means your neighbours can't disturb you with Cartoon Network. Amenities are basic, but the Castle Hill location is excellent. Rooms are twin not double.
16 rooms. $
Buda I, Szentháromság tér 6

Tel: 355-0122; Fax: 375-1886
e-mail: mka3@matavnet.hu

MEDOSZ

If you're looking for retro decor - twin beds set end to end, net curtains, shades of brown in all the fixtures and fittings, unsympathetic lighting - then this place is for you. Unrivalled location just off the main section of Andrássy út, next to Budapest's most happening square.
70 rooms. $
Pest VI, Jókai tér 9
Tel: 374-3000; Fax: 332-4316

PRIVATE ROOMS & PENSIONS

There are some reasonable town centre guesthouses - try, for example, City Panzió Pilvax (*Tel: 266 7660, www.taverna.hu*) - and some quieter suburban bed and breakfasts, such as the award-winning Beatrix Panzió (*Tel: 275 0550, www.beatrixhotel.hu*) in district II.

Private rooms can be booked through travel agencies, of which the main one is IBUSZ at Pest V, Ferenciek tere 10, *Tel: 485 2767*, and at Keleti Railway Station, *Tel 345 9572, e-mail accommodation@ibusz.hu* - both open working hours Monday to Friday only.

PRACTICAL TIPS

CULTURAL FESTIVALS

Budapest is rapidly creating a place for itself on the European cultural calendar. The Budapest Spring Festival in mid to late March is primarily a classical music festival but also has an arts and alternative side. It is worth booking in advance for big-name concerts, as Budapesters are avid concert-goers and tour groups also tend to make block bookings.

The Autumn Festival in late September focuses more on contemporary music and art, but has one or two major classical concerts as well, with early music also gaining ground.

Christmas is a family affair in Hungary, but the Lutheran Church on Deák tér always holds a free concert of Bach's *Christmas Oratorio*, and Handel's *Messiah* is performed in the Mátyás Church on Castle Hill. New Year's Eve (*Szilveszter* in Hungarian) sees people taking to the streets with hooters, whistles and firecrackers, ending up on Heroes' Square to sing the National Anthem.

For English-language listings of what's on, look in *WHERE Budapest,* a freebie carried by most upmarket hotels, or in *The Budapest Sun*, a weekly newspaper available in hotel lobbies or from news-stands. Other listings and information are available in *Budapest in Your Pocket*, which is carried by newspaper kiosks and selected outlets, for example Bestsellers bookshop at Pest V, Október 6. utca 11 and Vista Café at Pest VII, Paulay Ede utca 7.

PUBLIC TRANSPORT

Budapest transport is cheap, well-maintained and efficient. It was inspected recently as a potential model for the transport network of a 21st-century Japanese town. All forms of public transport require a ticket bought in advance - either at a metro station or news-stand - which you must punch into the ticket machines supplied on board trams, buses and trolley buses. In the case of the metro you must punch your ticket before you get on the escalator. Random spot-checks are carried out, especially on the metro, by inspectors sporting red and gold armbands. They will extract a fine

from you if you can't show a valid ticket. Trams always stop at every stop; on buses and trolley buses you must press the stop button by the doors if you want to get off. Public transport stops at 11.30, but there are night buses on most major routes. Note: If an older person or someone with young children gets on, you are expected to give up your seat for them. This is still common practice in Hungary. Watch out for pickpocket gangs who get on in a huddle, push and shout, cause a diversion, and then jump off at the next stop, laden with tourists' handbags.

If you take a taxi, don't jump into the first cab that comes along. Budapest taxis often take their passengers for a ride in more ways than one. Reputable companies are City Taxi (T: 211-1111); Fő Taxi (T: 222-2222) and Rádió Taxi (T: 377-7777). Phone rates are cheaper than street rates.

OPENING HOURS

Shops generally open at 10am, and close at 6pm. On Saturday afternoons, most shops are shut, and there is almost no Sunday opening, except for the new shopping malls. Banks tend to close at 4pm, but there are plenty of ATM machines around the city, and money-changing outlets stay open later, so access to cash should never be a problem. It is often worth getting an exchange rate quote from more than one bureau de change before parting with your hard currency, as rates do tend to differ from one to another.

LANGUAGE

Hungarian is one of the world's linguistic mysteries. No one knows quite where it came from; it is isolated in a sea of Slavic tongues, though is not Slavic itself; its closest relatives (and even they are not very close) are in faraway Finland and Siberia although there is a theory it is Turkic in origin.

Hungarians are proud of their uniqueness, and secretly quite like to believe that their language is unlearnable. Of course, it isn't: it is dauntingly unfamiliar at first, but it has an internal logic that ultimately puts a mongrel language like English to shame.

INDEX

Map References

NB: These grid references are for use with the colour map on pp. 190-191. Not all sights are marked individually on the map, but these references will guide you to street locations, or, in cases where the street is very long, to the relevant section of it.

PÓTVÁROS

Lehel tér

XIII

VÁCI ÚT

Nyugati tér

NYUGATI STATION

TERÉZ KRT.

KRT.

Nagymező

Jókai tér

Operetta Theatre

Liszt F. tér

WALK FIVE

Academy of Music

Új Színház

ANDRÁSSY

BAJCSY-ZSILINSZKY

Postal Mus.

Deák F. tér

Király

WALK EIGHT

Wesselényi

BELVÁROS

SYNAGOGUE

RÁKÓCZI

Dohány

Ferenciek tere

KOSSUTH L.U.

MUZEUM KRT.

WALK THREE

Széchenyi Sch.

NATIONAL MUSEUM

WALK FOUR

Kálvin tér

Baross

WALK SIX

Ráday

Fővám tér

VÁM

IX

SZABADSÁG BRIDGE

MUSEUM OF APPLIED ARTS

ÜLLŐI

ZSA GY.

Zoo

Museum of Fine Arts

Hősök tere

Museum of Agriculture

VAJDAHUNYAD CASTLE

Műcsarnok

C i t

p a r

ÚT

TERÉZVÁROS

Kodály körönd

Kodály Museum

VI

Király

ERZSÉBET

ERZSÉBETVÁROS

Madách Theatre

Wesselényi

VII

Dohány

KRT.

Blaha L. tér

Erkel Theatre

Köztársaság tér

Baross KER. STA.

tér

FIUMEI

Kere cem

JÓZSEF-

VI

JÓZSEF

ÚT

CITY OUTLINE

This map shows the eight walks in context. For a general city map with grid references, see pp. 190-191.

Sun. 23. 8.25 Check u.
Zita Stockwell, Arrival,
18.30. Drinks.
19.00. Concert,

Monday 24 10.0 Tour.
13.0 Lunch free.
16.30 Gala Dinner,
Church 10.00.
St. Mellenas
Tues. 25 optional.
10.30. State Opera House.
1.15 Meet lobby
6.30. State Opera Hse.
La Boheme.

Wed. 26
10.0 Lobby for Nat. Gallery.
Free hotel & P.M.
18.15 Lobby
Magic Flute.
Coach Return.
Thurs. Leave 8.45.
Lizt & Bartok.
12.15 Transfer
Airport.